ME, MY, MINE

*Perspectives on Recognizing and
Recovering from Narcissistic Abuse*

R.C. BLAKES, JR.

UNTAPPED POTENTIAL
PUBLISHING

UNTAPPED POTENTIAL
PUBLISHING

P.O. Box 84355, Pearland, TX 77584

"ME, MY, MINE"
*Perspectives on Recognizing and Recovering
from Narcissistic Abuse*

R.C. BLAKES, JR.

Printed in the United States of America First Printing 2022
First Edition 2022

ISBN: 978-0-9910868-8-7

10 9 8 7 6 5 4 3 2 1

Unless otherwise noted, Scripture quotations are
taken from the Holy Bible, King James Version.

DEDICATION

This book is dedicated to the millions of people who are victims of narcissistic abuse. My prayer is that this book opens your understanding, ushers in the healing power of God, and grants you freedom and wholeness in your soul.

This book is also dedicated to the many psychologists, therapists, and counselors who are in my circle and lend their invaluable counsel to me. You tolerate me and all my questions. Thank you for not writing off my perspective and encouraging me to produce this document.

Finally, this book is in honor of my most loyal social media family worldwide. If it were not for your overwhelming responses to all of my teachings on narcissism, I might have missed the great weight of this subject. Thank you for enlightening me

CONTENTS

INTRODUCTION

No one could have ever made me believe that I would be writing about the issues of narcissistic abuse, which seems to be an endless abyss of pain and trauma today for millions of people. Nearly three-fourths of the emails I receive are about some brand of narcissism and its impact on people's very real lives.

I initially stumbled into a study of the subject by mistake. I had written a book about soul ties (i.e., toxic relational bonds that seem impossible to break), and the correlation between the victims of soul ties and those victims of narcissistic abuse was uncanny. On certain points, the comparisons were so identical that people from the mental health community convinced me that I had just written a book about narcissistic abuse disorder (NAD) and the victim's struggle to break free. This took me by surprise. Who would have ever thought that I would be accused of addressing a topic so scientific? I am a simple preacher, a man, and a student of life. These are my credentials. I am not that smart.

The messages began to flood my email inbox and my office from people all around the world who were expressing their appreciation for haven helped them to overcome the narcissist. What?

This convinced me that I needed to do some research on the matter. I began to listen to psychologists and licensed professional counselors. I read articles about narcissism, and I began to see the connection.

What I Had Been Describing from a Biblical and Spiritual Perspective Was an Actual Psychological Reality.

With these enlightened eyes and expanded thought, I realized that I had been preaching and teaching about narcissism for decades. In fact, the character I describe in my earlier book, *The Father Daughter Talk*, is a classic narcissist. I even noticed that the Bible is replete with descriptions of narcissism in different terms.

IT WENT DEEPER

I started noticing the situations of the people I was counseling, who were in relationships, and the dots were connecting. Many of these people were narcissists and/or dealing with what appeared to be narcissism. I am always careful to render an internet diagnosis of a person because I am not authorized to do so. I am simply a student and a conscientious citizen of humanity. However, some of these cases are so blatant that my five-year-old grandson, Austin, could make the diagnosis.

My expanded consciousness on the subject broadened my theology and deepened my pastoral perspectives. I saw life, situations, and people more clearly. I realized how I had been the victim of religious narcissism all of my life. I saw how church people had manipulated and twisted my kindness for their own selfish agendas and discarded me and the church once they had accomplished their agenda. I began to notice the dynamic at work when I counseled couples. Either one or both were completely disinterested in the thoughts, feelings, or needs of the other and were completely obsessed with selfish gratification and impressions.

THE COUPLE FROM HELL

I remember doing a marital counseling session for this young couple. The session went on for hours. I remember thinking, "This is the couple from Hell." I don't literally mean that the people were from Hell or demonic; however, it is my humble opinion that something demonic was at work beneath the surface of this relationship. If you catch my drift, there was something spiritual, and it wasn't *Holy*. They would not listen to each other. They worked tirelessly to manipulate my opinion against the other. They heard nothing I said. They bullied each other and, at one point, appeared to develop energy for physical aggression. I had to literally stand between the two of them. In the course of the session, I learned that he carried an illegal firearm. It was time to go! After hours, we had gotten nowhere. I don't care what anybody says; these people were narcissists. I got them out of my office— never to return!

The most poignant revelations I got were in my assessment of relationships. The idea of people being so attached to some toxic love interest, to the point of self-denial and even self-destruction, had a more crystalized meaning. I began to see the effects of narcissistic abuse and how the trauma generated an emptying of the victim's self-worth, thereby creating a toxic addiction to the abuser and the need for that abuser's approval, which never comes.

As I was getting an education as a middle-aged preacher, I began to see a seamless connection between the spiritual and the scientific. Nobody taught this at Bible college or seminary. The Bible that I have read all of my life has always addressed these issues in tones and in a language of antiquity. The modern psychological concepts and terms were simply a spin on ancient issues.

I started to create videos on social media about the narcissist. As I learned something, I would share it with my audience. The demand became greater and greater for these conversations.

This book is an acknowledgment of my expanded consciousness. It is my contribution to the healing of a generation that has been so severely damaged by these very sad people called narcissists. As diabolical as they are, they are simply reflecting the internal pain that life has heaped upon them in one way or another. This is not to give you the idea that you may rescue them from their pain. I believe that would be a psychological trap. All you may do for them is acknowledge who they are, accept their reality, and move forward without the need for the closure you desire from them. They cannot give it to you. All you may do for them is leave them in the hands of God. For them, life is *Me, Myself, and I*—anybody else is either a tool or an inconvenience.

CHAPTER 1

WHAT

IS

A

NARCISSIST

If you were to ask me what a narcissist was some years ago, I would have told you that a narcissist is simply an ego-driven, self-consumed person. That is not wrong, but it's extremely incomplete and overly simplistic. There's nothing simple about a narcissist. The sad truth is that this narrow view would represent most people's opinions. As a society, we are incredibly undereducated about narcissistic abuse. This level of ignorance in this matter is very dangerous. To have such a narrow view of such a dangerous dynamic is like going into the jungle with no knowledge of the animals or vegetation. At any moment, one may be poisoned to death or consumed by a predator because of a lack of knowledge.

The Bible describes the tragedy that ensues when one lacks sufficient knowledge. The Bible says in HOSEA 4:6, *My people are destroyed for lack of knowledge: because thou hast rejected knowledge, I will also reject thee, that thou shalt be no priest to me: seeing thou hast forgotten the law of thy God, I will also forget thy children.*

The text enlightens us of the fact that a lack of knowledge can render a person destroyed, and it may paralyze the next generation. In other words, your children may suffer because of your missteps.

A narcissist is more than a person consumed with his or her looks or selfishness. If it were that simple, that description would describe the majority of those living in the United States and Europe. Narcissism goes much deeper. Narcissism is a factor in lands where no fancy cars and mansions can be had. It is a universal, cross-cultural plague.

THE MYTHOLOGICAL CHARACTER NARCISSUS

The term *narcissist* is lifted from the Greek mythological character named Narcissus. Narcissus was a handsome young hunter who one day gazed in a still pond and saw his reflection. Narcissus fell in love with his image and overdosed on admiring himself and filling his self-talk with constant self-adoration. As the myth goes, he would speak to his image and say, "I love you." He did this until he eventually died.

This is where we gather such a minute concept of narcissism. When we fail to look deeper, we conclude that it is merely self-indulgence. The realities are hidden because Narcissus could not focus on or see anyone else but himself. His mind was so severely damaged that he perceived no reality outside himself. Ultimately, we see the depth of narcissism in that Narcissus actually died because of his vanity.

NARCISSISM IS MORE THAN COMMON VANITY

When you really stop and think about it, narcissism has to be more than vanity. All of us are vain to one degree or another. We all have selfish moments and feelings. To call one a narcissist means a great deal more than selfish behavior from time to time.

My definition of a narcissist: An extremely self-centered person who has an exaggerated sense of self-importance and grandiosity and has no sense of empathy.

A person with a narcissistic personality disorder has a deeper issue than one who is simply on an ego trip or having a selfish episode. This person demonstrates at least one or more of the characteristics listed in the above definition. I'm certain that the potential characteristics go far beyond my list, but this is my limited perspective.

The individual will exhibit extreme self- centeredness. This trait will be alarming because it will resemble the selfish behavior of a toddler who demands to have his way at any cost. The major difference is that it would manifest in a person of age who should understand social rules, compromise, and boundaries. It would be as strange as observing a grown, bearded man sitting in the middle of a floor, pouting to have his way.

The individual is so consumed and enamored with himself that it is nauseating. They never see a mirror they don't like. They never miss an opportunity to toot their own horn, and they take every occasion to declare their own greatness. They can go on and on about themselves for hours and never discern their audience's boredom or repulsion.

The narcissist is sometimes very grandiose. In other words, certain kinds of narcissists develop an impressive style. Image becomes paramount. They buy cars that signify money. Labels and brands are a necessity, and they communicate to the general public that they are living a high life. They compete with everyone else, and it's important for them to feel like they have won. They might actually say: "I'm a winner, and you're a loser."

The most tragic and universal characteristic of narcissists is their inability to feel empathy. The most basic definition of empathy is the human ability to put one's self in another person's shoes, especially when they are feeling pain. It is the human tendency to relate to how certain events, behavior, or activity might make another person feel. Anything less is uncivilized.

A Narcissist Has No Connection to Other People's Feelings, Nor Do They Have Concern.

Normal, well-adjusted people always consider how other people are being made to feel. Jesus demonstrated empathy for us. The Bible says in HEBREWS 4:15, *For we have not a high priest that cannot be touched with the feeling of our infirmities; but one that hath been in all points tempted like as we are, yet without sin.*

Jesus had never sinned, but he could identify with our feelings as sinners. He had an empathetic capacity. Narcissists do not have this ability. Their worldview does not consist of other people being important besides being useful for supplying their needs.

As we will discuss in the pages ahead, these various characteristics are probably linked to the type of narcissist the person is. There are different types, as we will discuss later.

THE REALITY OF NARCISSISM IS ANCIENT; THE STUDY IS CONTEMPORARY

According to Kendra Cherry and Dr. Steven Glans in their article "Very Well Mind," the scholarly psychological study of narcissism is fairly young—maybe less than a century. It was around the late 1970s to 1980s that NPD (narcissistic personality disorder) was officially listed.

In as much as the scientific acknowledgment of NPD is fairly contemporary, the Bible demonstrates narcissism before the creation of man.

I suppose every person, coming from their particular vantage point, could create an argument based on their context. My vantage point is spiritual, Christian, and biblical. If you are coming from another position, do not get lost in my perspective and abandon the greater value of this entire discussion. We are going to the same destination from different routes.

As I searched for the earliest point where I could identify narcissism, it took me back—way before the 1900s. In fact, I found a record of narcissistic personality predating the world and humanity. Narcissism was here before we were.

Lucifer is the Father of Narcissism

The name Lucifer is another moniker for the one we call Satan or the Devil. Before he got these other handles, God called him Lucifer.

Lucifer was an archangel in Heaven—a chief angel who led a large congregation of angels. His particular talent was music, and he was described as a beautiful creature. His assignment was to lead the worship of God, but one day he got caught up in pride and developed an inflated view of himself. He saw himself above God.

The word says in ISAIAH 14:12-14, *How art thou fallen from heaven, O Lucifer, son of the morning! how art thou cut down to the ground, which didst weaken the nations! For thou hast said in thine heart, I will ascend into heaven, I will exalt my throne above the stars of God: I will sit also upon the mount of the congregation, in the sides of the north: I will ascend above the heights of the clouds; I will be like the Most- High.*

A Narcissist Always Has to Be Better Than Others

If you research the entire biblical account of Lucifer, you'll discover that he overestimated himself and desired to be equal to the Most-High God. Like the Greek mythological figure Narcissus, Lucifer was blinded by his image and toxic self-love. I believe Lucifer is the father of the narcissistic spirit that prevails today. This is my spiritual opinion as a minister and pastor.

The Totality of Narcissism Transcends a Mere Mental Disorder; I Believe it is Spiritual in its Essence and Origin.

The Apostle Paul wrote to his young protégé, Timothy, about avoiding a certain kind of person. This person would have the temperament of cancer.

It is recorded in 2 TIMOTHY 3:1–7, *This know also, that in the last days perilous times shall come. For men shall be lovers of their own selves, covetous, boasters, proud, blasphemers, disobedient to parents, unthankful, unholy, without natural affection, trucebreakers, false accusers, incontinent, fierce, despisers of those that are good, Traitors, heady, high-minded, lovers of pleasures more than lovers of God; Having a form of godliness but denying the power thereof: from such turn away. For of this sort are they which creep into houses, and lead captive silly women laden with sins, led away with divers lusts, Ever learning, and never able to come to the knowledge of the truth.* 2 TIMOTHY 3:1-7 Describes the Complexities of Narcissistic Disorder.

If you were to take a psychology textbook that describes narcissistic personality disorder and compare the textbook with Paul's biblical description in this letter to Timothy, you would think that Paul must have lifted his thoughts from a psychology textbook. When Paul penned these descriptions, it was before the science of psychology existed, and it predates the concepts of narcissism by thousands of years. On a spiritual level, I believe that narcissism is the spirit of Lucifer, creating the same sense of self-worship within humankind that Lucifer exhibited pre-creation.

Narcissism Had a Spiritual Root Before It Was Recognized as a Psychological Disorder.

Let us not make the same mistake frequently made, which is to characterize everybody who is difficult as being a narcissist. Every time we see a selfish, manipulative person, it does not necessarily reflect a narcissist. Some people simply have character issues, and sometimes we catch the person on a bad day. There is a definite difference between narcissism and being narcissistic.

The fact is this: We all can be narcissistic. There are times when we are more consumed with self-advancement, selfish needs, and self- interest than others. This happens for several reasons. The difference between a normal person and one who might be legitimately characterized as a narcissist is this: Normal people have these narcissistic episodes and correct their behavior once they come to themselves. In other words, all persons may have a selfish moment or inclination. Most people are capable of recognizing their behavior and adjusting themselves; it's just a fleeting episode. This is not an episode for a real narcissist —the character they display is actually who they are at their core. They are consistently evil and deceptive.

A Narcissist Does Not Possess the Ability to Correct Their Selfishness. They Live on this Frequency Continuously.

There are many people who do terrible things and later repent for their antics. This person, in my humble opinion, is no narcissist. They simply represent the broad spectrum of emotions and behavior that makes one human.

A narcissist does not possess the depth to see the need for repentance. A narcissist may be sorry for being caught in a certain act, but they will never truly be repentant. If being sorry repositions the narcissist to continue taking advantage, they will be sorry.

It reminds me of the character Eddie Murphy played in the movie *The Nutty Professor*. He was the slim and handsome alter ego of the overweight professor, Professor Klump; Buddy was his name. Buddy was going on a date with the beautiful, young, female professor, played by Jada Pinkett Smith. When Buddy arrived in his flashy sports car and fancy clothes, he dropped to one knee and pleaded for forgiveness. As soon as it was apparent that his act worked to regain her affection, he immediately went back to the brash egomaniac he was. He was sorry but never repentant. His sorrow was necessary to regain his position.

Psychologists Say That a Narcissist Cannot Repent.

I must admit that I am still pondering the idea that a narcissist cannot repent. As a minister, I am always of the persuasion that a person may have an encounter with God that can break him and bring him to repentance. I also have to admit that I have not seen one who exhibits the characteristics of a bona fide narcissist change. Even in scripture, we look at Lucifer, who has never repented. We see Jezebel, another biblical example of a narcissist who never repented. Even Judas, the one who betrayed Jesus, never repented. Of course, the jury is out on Judas really being a narcissist or not. Some say he was a narcissist, while others say he was not because he exhibited sorrow when he discovered that Jesus would be crucified because of his actions. But note that he didn't get sorrowful until he realized they were going to actually kill Jesus. He was so sorrowful he committed suicide (MATTHEW 27:1–10). The questions remain: Was Judas sorry for what he had done to Jesus, like a normal person would be, or was he sorry that his actions had now brought an end to life as he had known? Judas was the treasurer for the most popular man in Israel. He held high status. This would no longer be the case. Was he sorry that his name would now be the equivalent to that of mud and that someone would probably kill him for what he had done? These are honest questions.

I can't say what drove Judas' choices in his final hours, but a narcissist can become so self-pitying about the personal impact of his bad behavior that it drives him to suicide.

I find it interesting that Judas was so sorry that he killed himself, but he made no attempt to talk with Jesus. He didn't even send a word. Was he sorry about what he had done and its impact on Jesus, or was he lamenting how his actions changed his personal life?

Narcissists Do Not Have the Ability to Decipher Right from Wrong

The word says in ROMANS 1:28–31, *And even as they did not like to retain God in their knowledge, God gave them over to a reprobate mind, to do those things which are not convenient; Being filled with all unrighteousness, fornication, wickedness, covetousness, maliciousness; full of envy, murder, debate, deceit, malignity; whisperers, Backbiters, haters of God, despiteful, proud, boasters, inventors of evil things, disobedient to parents, Without understanding, covenant-breakers, without natural affection, implacable, unmerciful.*

When we look at this text, we see a laundry list of characteristics that may translate into any Psych 101 course. The term *reprobate*, specifically in this text, may be defined as *one who lacks the ability to discern right from wrong*. This definition captures the spirit of a narcissist. They are oblivious to any core sense of righteousness.

They discern nothing outside of self-gratification. They do not feel your pain and therefore are never truly sorry for their part in it.

WHAT IS THE NARCISSIST IN PRACTICAL, EVERYDAY TERMS?

THE NARCISSIST IS AN EMOTIONAL VAMPIRE

They take and consume love and affection that they will never replenish. They drain their victims of everything, from money to sex and time. They consume their victims like the mythical vampire does its prey.

Their constitution won't allow them to reciprocate love because they are consumed with self-interest, self-image, or self-preservation; a narcissist cannot actually return love authentically. They are sometimes capable of acting for brief stints if it will afford them something they desire or need from their victim, but they cannot love you back. They are like the mythical Greek character we just discussed, Narcissus, who was so obsessed with gazing upon his image that he could see no one else but himself.

It matters not how much you do to prove your loyalty and love; the narcissist recognizes none of it, and they will never return you the same sentiment.

You Cannot Love a Narcissist Enough to Change Their Nature.

This also reinforces my belief that narcissism originates with Lucifer as a spiritual curse. As much as the Almighty loved and esteemed Lucifer, Lucifer's heart was irreparable. He was incapable of returning a comparable response of love and loyalty.

This is most difficult to accept when you are coming from a healthy place of empathy and human compassion. A narcissist's inability to return your affection can make you feel like something is wrong with you. It has nothing to do with you. They will take what they can and never return.

A person cannot give you what they do not possess. The narcissist has the uncanny ability to bring your mood down into the dumps. Depression seems to accompany their arrival, and you feel yourself sliding into a dark place because of them.

Their words and even their text messages just drain the energy and enthusiasm from your life. It's like a bad drug addiction; every time you crash, you ask yourself, "Why am I still dealing with this?"

The Prophet Elijah experienced the vampire-like effect the narcissist can have on a person's spirit. It was after he defeated Jezebel's false prophets, and she simply sent him a word. Those words were so diabolical they drove Elijah into a depression. He actually articulated wanting to die. He was coming off of his greatest victory, and yet life was drained from him by a simple communication between him and Jezebel. A narcissist can drain the living out of life.

The account of Elijah and Jezebel is found in 1 KINGS 19:2–3, which says, *Then Jezebel sent a messenger unto Elijah, saying, So let the gods do to me, and more also, if I make not thy life as the life of one of them by tomorrow about this time. And when he saw that, he arose, and went for his*

*life, and came to Beersheba, which belongeth to Judah, and
left his servant there.*

Elijah got this threat from Jezebel and immediately
started running for his life. Her message brought him into
panic and depression. She drained the life from him when
he should have been most thrilled.

THE NARCISSIST IS AN ACTOR

The narcissist is attracted to people who are needy or
eager for a relationship. They then create a character to
match the profile of the victim's desires. It's only an act.
They are playing a role for a selfish payoff.

Narcissists Are Fundamentally
Programmed Against Relationships

Not only does the narcissist not know how to reciprocate love,
but they are not equipped to participate in a relationship.
They will embrace the semblance of a relationship to
position themselves for advancement or manipulation, but
they will never be a full participant in a real relationship.

A relationship requires the maturity to consider the
needs and expectations of another person. The true narcissist
cannot connect to the concept of a relationship. They will
always disappoint. They disappoint their parents, spouses,
siblings, and even children. They are too emotionally shallow
to facilitate a relationship. They will always fail the other
person's expectations.

One of the most prevalent examples of what it looks
like when a narcissist is playing a role is in the strip clubs

of America. There you'll find young and beautiful women convincing old, fat guys that they still have it. The purpose of this scene is to get the money out of the old guy's pocket and onto the stage. It's just an act.

There's a biblical record of a certain type of person who manipulates for personal gain. It is found in PROVERBS 6:24–26, which says: *To keep thee from the evil woman, from the flattery of the tongue of a strange woman. Lust not after her beauty in thine heart; neither let her take thee with her eyelids. For by means of a whorish woman a man is brought to a piece of bread: and the adulteress will hunt for the precious life.*

Notice how this woman is described as being beautiful, flirtatious, and flattering, but when she is done, her victim is destroyed. She made the poor little man believe she loved and was attracted to him. It was an act, and the scene came to an abrupt and horrific end.

The narcissist will tell you exactly what you want to hear until they have positioned you in a place of vulnerability and codependence. Flattery is one of their greatest weapons.

THE NARCISSIST IS AN OPPORTUNIST

According to Siri, "An opportunist is one who exploits circumstances to gain an immediate advantage rather than being guided by consistent principles."

The narcissist is the ultimate opportunist. They are always looking at angles that will serve their advancement. They excel in positions of power, like politics, ministry, and business. Wherever a political system determines promotion, they usually do well. They will cut anyone's throat and stoop to any level to access an opportunity. The Apostle Paul describes the tactics of Satan in 2 CORINTHIANS 2:11: *Lest Satan should get an advantage of us: for we are not ignorant of his devices.* The narcissist is like a wrestler. They are always jockeying for the upper hand. Once they get the advantage, they take complete control of the opportunity to use you for their promotion. After they are done, they will then discard you like a wastepaper. The narcissist is an opportunist.

While They Are Your Priority, You Are for Them Just an Option and Opportunity

When we look at the most popular of biblical narcissists, Jezebel, we see the opportunistic nature of a narcissist. Narcissists do not usually participate in relationships without it supplying them with something they want and/ or need. Jezebel was really powerless. She used Ahab, her husband and king, to facilitate her wickedness. Ahab was her supply of power, prestige, and intimidation.

The Bible says in 1 KINGS 16:31–32, *And it came to pass, as if it had been a light thing for him to walk in the sins of Jeroboam the son of Nebat, that he took to wife Jezebel the daughter of Ethbaal king of the Zidonians, and went and served Baal, and worshipped him. And he reared up an altar for Baal in the house of Baal, which he had built in Samaria.*

This is the record of Ahab taking Jezebel as his wife. The Bible equates it to sin. His marriage to Jezebel led to idolatry prevailing in the land. Ahab was nothing more than narcissistic supply. Jezebel needed power and authority, and she took the opportunity to supply that by marrying the weak Ahab.

A NARCISSIST IS AN ASSASSIN

A narcissist is the most ruthless of enemies. When they have it out for you, there is nothing they won't do. It requires great wisdom to detangle yourself from the narcissist. We will discuss how to do this in a later chapter.

A narcissist is unforgiving, relentless, unforgetting, and ruthless when they feel a need to get even or attack a person. Though the narcissist may be physically dangerous, in most cases, they do damage to their victim's self-esteem and public reputation. They are usually triggered by anyone who threatens their comfort zone or their public image. They can go from lamb to lion when they feel like their territory is being infringed upon.

Jezebel sought to murder Elijah when he destroyed her image of power and dominance. She had to bring him down to build herself up. Jezebel sent her false prophets to engage in a public battle with Elijah to prove whose God was more powerful. Elijah defeated all of her false prophets and idols. This public embarrassment infuriated Jezebel. Her flunky, King Ahab, brought her the report.

The Bible records in 1 KINGS 19:1-2, *And Ahab told Jezebel—all that Elijah had done, and—withal how he had slain—all the prophets with the sword. Then Jezebel sent a messenger unto Elijah, saying, So let the gods do to me, and more also, if I make not—thy life as the life of one of them by tomorrow about this time.*

Her wrath was drawn to Elijah because he embarrassed her by defeating her publicly.

Public Embarrassment Brings the Worst Out of a Narcissist.

There's an interesting passage of scripture found in PROVERBS 22:24–25, and it says: *Make no friendship with an angry man; and with a furious man thou shalt not go: Lest thou learn his ways and get a snare to thy soul.*

The wisdom of this proverb is that it's best to avoid being in a relationship with someone with a propensity for anger. When it says, "Lest thou learn his ways," that could mean one of two things: (1) You will pick up on bad habits, or (2) you will see a side of this individual you did not know was there. I believe that both of these scenarios are true. You don't really know how far a person can go until you see them in certain circumstances.

THE NARCISSIST IS AN EMOTIONAL TODDLER

Finally, a narcissist is often a parent or even a grandparent with the emotional intelligence of a toddler. This is especially evident when you are dealing with the grandiose type. They almost behave like a child at the school play: "Look at me!"

From what I have learned about narcissists, they struggle from arrested development created by several factors. Though their bodies have aged, their consciousness is stuck in a broken childhood. They may be a fifty-year-old person on the calendar and yet are emotionally stuck in grade school, fighting for attention and recognition.

It Is Frustrating to Deal with a Narcissist Because It Is Like Interacting with a Child.

The Apostle Paul discusses a similar frustration, on a spiritual level, with the Corinthian Church.

He says to them in 1 CORINTHIANS 3:1–4, *And I, brethren, could not speak unto you as unto spiritual, but as unto carnal, even as unto babes in Christ. I have fed you with milk, and not with meat: for hitherto ye were not able to bear it, neither yet now are ye able. For ye are yet carnal: for whereas there is among you envying, and strife, and divisions,are ye not carnal, and walk as men? For while one saith, I am of Paul; and another, I am of Apollos; are ye not carnal?*

Though Paul was speaking of the spiritual immaturity of the church, he describes their characteristics as being envious, strifeful, and divisive. These are the childish tendencies of a narcissist.

A Narcissist Can Turn a Boardroom into a Nursery School Playpen.

Sometimes the language becomes so primary it may become overwhelming. This is when the hurt little child surfaces.

CHAPTER 2

THE

BREEDING

OF

A

NARCISSIST

The million-dollar question is: Where do narcissists come from? Are they simply demon spawns? Are they born this way?

This was my burning question when I was awakened to the reality that a narcissist is more than an arrogant or conceited person. When I began to comprehend the depth of depravity involved with a person who is truly a narcissist, I wondered: What makes a person so diabolical and vile?

To some extent, it is a mystery. It's a mystery to me how Lucifer could have done what he did. How could he have been lifted up by pride and rebellion? As good as God had been to him, how could Lucifer attempt to usurp God's glory? The irony is that even God seemed to be puzzled by the lunacy of Lucifer's breakdown.

God asked Lucifer an interesting question in ISAIAH 14:12: *How art thou fallen from heaven, O Lucifer, son of the morning! how art thou cut down to the ground, which didst weaken the nations!*

God is asking Lucifer, "What are you doing? What makes you forfeit everything I've graced you with to self-destruct in this egocentric meltdown? Why?"

Isn't this the question many of us ask when we see people displaying severe narcissistic behavior that ultimately hurts them as much as it does everyone else?

Narcissistic psychology will never add up on the surface. If you are a rational and remotely well-adjusted person, you will never comprehend a narcissist and their actions. However, there are real reasons why these people exist, and why they have been emotionally transfigured into the sad and hurtful beings they are.

LOOK DEEPER

A friend of mine was on vacation in Africa. She took a video of some rocks by the ocean. She instructed us to look closely at the video, and we would see little crabs crawling on the rocks. If you had just glanced at the video without looking deeper, you would have only seen the obvious. The truth was that there was more than apparent. There was activity happening within the obvious activity.

There are many realities in life that simply require a deeper perspective. Think about the millions of stars that are presently existing all around you. You cannot see them with your naked eye. When you utilize the power and perspective of a telescope, it allows you to look deeper into the Cosmos and behold realities that would escape you otherwise.

One of the perspectives that helps us to see the soul of a narcissist is psychology. I am from the spiritual/religious community, and there are things that we understand; however, psychologists, in my opinion, give us some very helpful insight into the origins of a narcissist, how they are formed and how to manage them when necessary.

This is one of the things I have studied and learned from some of the mental health professionals that do a great job of educating the public on narcissistic abuse disorder.

One of the most important facts to always consider is that everybody has a narcissistic trait. We all may be selfish. We are all jerks at times. In other words, as we've discussed, you and I, at multiple times in our lives, will behave with a narcissistic twist. It's when the ego gets the best of us. The narcissist is stuck in that cycle. Narcissism has a wide range. We see narcissistic tendencies in a baby, naturally wanting to have its way, to the sociopath who devastates an entire community. There's the potential for narcissistic reflexes within us all.

According to the Mayo Clinic, these are the signs associated with narcissistic personality disorder: an exaggerated sense of self-importance, a sense of entitlement, feelings of superiority, exaggerated achievements, preoccupation with fantasies about success, ideas of superiority over others and being too good for certain people, monopolization of conversations, belief that they deserve unquestioned compliance, taking advantage of others to get what they want, no recognition of the needs of others, envy and belief they are envied by others, boastfulness, and always wanting the best available.

According to the American Psychiatric Association's *Diagnostic and Statistical Manual of Mental Disorders* (DSM-5), a person will display five or more of the previously listed characteristics to be diagnosed by a professional mental health worker as a narcissist.

Though there is scientific evidence that certain people may be born with a chemical composition that makes them prone to narcissistic personality disorder, most mental health professionals agree that most narcissists develop due to poor or no parenting.

WHERE DO NARCISSISTS COME FROM?

1. TRAUMATIC CHILDHOOD PARENTING

I believe many psychologists would concur that most narcissists are bred through poor and abusive parenting. In other words, the narcissist has been raised to self-obsess by the kind of parenting they've been exposed to. The narcissist has often been socialized by their parents. If not parents, those who were guardians of the young soul have created an emotional wound that may never heal.

The Narcissist Is Often the Product of Childhood Trauma.

Many narcissists are people who have never recovered from their childhood and are now locked into a destructive and dysfunctional identity, devoid of empathy and consumed with self-gratification. The narcissist is a broken little child locked inside a grown person's frame. These statements are not to generate any futile hope that you may save the narcissist from their childhood pain. That line of thought can be super commendable but seriously self-destructive. The issues are too personal and complex to manage for anyone short of a mental health professional. In fact, many mental health professionals may find their expertise neutralized in a personal relationship with a narcissist. They may have all of the know-how and understand the therapeutic process and still be pulled into their emotions, forsaking their skills. As a minister, I have had countless therapists and psychologists reach out to me in confidence that they were being devastated by a relationship with a narcissist. This is one reason I believe that there's more to the narcissist than twisted psychology—there's something seriously spiritual.

Feeling emotional empathy for a narcissist and taking the risk of sacrificing yourself to save them is like driving through the bush in Africa and getting out of your vehicle to free a full-grown lion trapped in a maze of thorns. You won't get gratitude and love from the lion; you will get the brunt of the lion's nature. You meant well, but the story ends with you being the lunch the rescued lion.

The narcissist is created by abusive parenting. The first type of parenting that breeds a narcissist is the parent who traumatizes their child. This is the parent that withholds affection, uses comparisons to humiliate the child, sexually abuses the child, physically abuses the child, and whatever other abusive act you can think of.

An Abusive Parent Is an Emotional Vampire That Drains the Hopes, Dreams, and Self-Esteem of the Abused Child.

Being abused by the very person that the child is forced to rely on to protect, defend and provide for them only serves to emotionally and psychologically isolate and terrorize the child. The child is like a cornered cat that has to tap into its most virile instincts to survive. This brings the most violent reaction out of the cat.

Think about a child in this same position day in and day out at the hands of a predatory parent. What is a response to a hostile moment for average people becomes the absolute norm for a child raised by a predator. There are kids who are raised in environments where they do not have a moment of security or affirmation.

The constant abuse, tension, and disapproval create a groove in the child's subconscious mind that won't let them escape the concept of "me against the world." It's like a scratch on a vinyl record that is stuck in an annoying loop.

The child who lives through childhood trauma at the hands of a caretaker goes inside their own head. Within that inner world, they formulate a safe relationship with themselves. Their internal world is an escape from their reality. They see their real self as worthless, so they create a character in their head. They then begin to locate what is necessary to manifest this alternate version of themselves. Because they've been conditioned to hate themselves and have a high need to be loved and accepted, they do whatever and use whomever to underwrite their empty sense of self-worth. Quite often, the false self that the narcissist creates is extraverted and grand. It is the polar opposite of the real, insecure or fearful self. The real self is thought of as unattractive and undesirable. This false persona is always presented as better than everyone else.

The Grandiose Persona Is Really the Cover for the Inner Child's Private Feelings of Inferiority and Powerlessness.

The unfortunate reality is that the narcissist quite often discovers a social structure that supports their grandiose façade. They are then encouraged by external stimuli that their internal chaos is right and profitable. This perpetuates the façade and cements the false self into place. The world tends to respond favorably to people who appear to be strong, decisive, and successful. The narcissist finds great profit and comfort within their false identity.

2. CHILDHOOD IDOLIZATION

Another factor that often breeds a narcissist is childhood idolization. When a parent or community builds a child up to believe that they are the center of the universe, the child internalizes this obsessive worship and takes it to a very toxic and socially dysfunctional level. The child is mentally programmed to believe that the world should serve his every desire. This is the common problem with childhood stars: They don't know how to separate the fame and attention they receive for their craft from reality. In the real world, there are laws and social boundaries that must be recognized. When the child experiences resistance, they don't know how to process it. This sometimes leads to drug abuse and even stints in jail.

Usually, Parents Who Idolize Are Oblivious to the Psychological Damage They Are Doing to Their Child.

There's an actual case within my extended family where a child had been idolized as she had been raised. I won't give too many details for obvious reasons. The child was idolized and considered better than the other children in the same family.

When the child came to adulthood, the child's development had been so arrested that she refused to maintain steady employment, committed certain crimes, spent time in jail, and abused drugs. In the meantime, the other children became productive contributors to society. The idolized child sought to live off of the other siblings, who were supposed to be beneath her. This included begging for money, stealing, and other activities. This person could not grasp the idea of personal responsibility. Today she is an older woman, and she lives as if the world owes her everything. It's incredible to observe. I am no mental health professional, but I dare say she is a narcissist.

When A Child Has Been Idolized, It Leads to A Delusional and Dysfunctional Sense of Superiority.

The inner child is trapped within the false reality of idolization and can never come to terms with the fact that the world owes them nothing. They may grow up, but inwardly they see themselves on little thrones barking orders that must be obeyed. It is a sad scene to watch. It's even more horrific for the relatives and friends dealing with this adult-child's arrested development and warped sense of reality.

Child Idolization in The Bible

There's a biblical record of a case of child idolization. It is the story of Jacob (also known as Israel) and his son Joseph. Joseph was a child that was born in Jacob's older years. The fact that he was conceived in Jacob's twilight years made Joseph special to Jacob. His love for Joseph became problematic when Jacob made no effort to conceal his preference for Joseph from Joseph's brothers. Joseph had eleven other brothers, and his father blatantly loved him more than all of them. As I ponder this biblical text from a psychological perspective, I think we can also see how his toxic parenting created trauma, which manifested in a more malignant fashion in certain of his other sons. Jacob's overt favor for Joseph created hatred in the other brothers for Joseph, which manifested in them considering killing Joseph.

The Bible records this pitiful example of parenting in GENESIS 37:3–4: *Now Israel loved Joseph more than all his children, because he was the son of his old age: and he made him a coat of many colors. And when his brethren saw that their father loved him more than all his brethren, they hated him, and could not speak peaceably unto him.*

The Bible is as direct about Jacob's idolization of Joseph as it can possibly be. He loved Joseph more than all of his other children. It's no wonder that Joseph's brothers hated him. Their father humiliated them by idolizing their younger brother.

While Jacob Was Idolizing Their Brother, He Was Traumatizing the Rest of His Children.

Though I do not believe Joseph to have been a narcissist on any level, I do believe that this story shows us a parapraxis with Joseph. According to *Merriam-Webster*, a parapraxis is an unconscious statement, spoken or written, that stems from a subconscious line of thought. In other words, it is something that slips out in speech, which reveals a deeper trend of thinking or attitude within the individual. This is more commonly known as a Freudian slip.

I think that the Bible shows us such a slip with Joseph. Many theologians will not agree with my assessment because we Christians think of our biblical heroes as flawless and faultless. Personally, I believe that biblical heroes are poignant and significant because they were flawed and human, like us. The power of God is not revealed in the idea of them being perfect; the power of God is revealed in the fact that they were clearly imperfect.

Joseph makes a statement to his brothers that was divinely inspired and humanly foolish all at the same time. When we look at it, I believe that we will see the beginnings of the effects of idolization coming out in his choice of words.

The story continues in GENESIS 37:5–11: *And Joseph dreamed a dream, and he told it his brethren: and they hated him yet the more. And he said unto them, Hear, I pray you, this dream which I have dreamed: For, behold, we were binding sheaves in the field, and, lo, my sheaf arose, and also stood upright; and, behold, your sheaves stood round about, and made obeisance to my sheaf. And his brethren said to him, Shalt thou indeed reign over us? or shalt thou indeed have dominion over us? And they hated him yet the more for his dreams, and for his words.*

And he dreamed yet another dream, and told it his brethren, and said, Behold, I have dreamed a dream more; and, behold, the sun and the moon and the eleven stars made obeisance to me. And he told it to his father, and to his brethren: and his father rebuked him, and said unto him, what is this dream that thou hast dreamed? Shall I and thy mother and thy brethren indeed come to bow down ourselves to thee to the earth? And his brethren envied him; but his father observed the saying.

In this text, we see that Joseph has an authentic dream from God; we cannot deny the dream because it did come to pass. *The thing I want you to consider is the fact that Joseph had a mind to communicate the dream to his family and the words he chose to communicate it. Joseph was comfortable saying to his family that they would bow in submission and inferiority to him one day. What would make Joseph tell anybody that God showed him this? The Bible does not say that God told Joseph to communicate this dream. Why would Joseph not be conscious enough to know that the words he chose would incite his family?*

I submit this theory to you: Joseph's reality had been shaped by the idolization of his father, Jacob. To Joseph, it may have seemed perfectly normal to conceive of a world where he was superior and his brothers were inferior. His choice of words did not register as condescending or intolerable to him because he lived in a reality of idolization. It was normal for him to be worshipped and superior to his brothers.

When you read the rest of the story, you will see how God brought Joseph from a father who was idolizing him into a polar opposite reality. The story continues like this:

His brothers sold him into slavery, lied to their father, and said he was eaten by a wild beast. He became a slave and eventually a prisoner. He was forgotten and abandoned.

The Best Things May Come from
the Worst Experiences.

I personally believe that it was divine providence that separated Joseph from his father. On the surface, it looks like it was purely the jealousy of his siblings. If we look deeper, we may conclude that God orchestrated the entire situation to save Joseph's soul (mind) before he would be completely formed into a full-blown narcissist (one without empathy or consideration for others).

When you read the story, you'll see how God allowed the exact opposite of idolization to become Joseph's new reality. He went from idolization to humiliation. I believe that all of this was to humble him and to balance his soul. God forced Joseph to feel his brothers' reality.

Later, Joseph himself acknowledges the personal benefit of the suffering God allowed him to endure. The story of Joseph is an amazing story. Joseph goes from slave to prison to the second most powerful man beside Pharaoh.

Later, when there's a famine in the land, Joseph's brothers actually have to come to Egypt for food, and they, unknowingly kneel before Joseph. When he makes them aware that he is their brother Joseph, he says to them in GENESIS 50:20, what you meant for evil God meant it for good".

Sometimes Separation Is Protection.

It was good that Joseph had been separated from his toxic father. It was good that God balanced him out with hardship and servitude. Childhood idolization could have very well destroyed Joseph's destiny. Many narcissists are created through childhood idolization.

3. CODDLING A CAPABLE PERSON

This may sound similar to idolization, but it is a little different, in my opinion. Sometimes people are coddled by those closest to them for reasons other than idolization. Sometimes people are coddled because they are viewed as incapable of doing for themselves.

In this case, the community surrounding the young child does everything for the kid, and nothing changes as the kid slowly grows into adolescence. The overly helpful mother refuses to allow the son to exercise any independence. The protective father spoils the daughter beyond reason. This continues into the teen years, and eventually, we have a full-grown adult who has no survival skills. This leads to a grown person who becomes a drain on society. He uses everyone around him to meet his basic needs. She was never given the skills of independence and self-reliance. This is a parenting error.

Stage-Appropriate Parenting Is Necessary

There is stage-appropriate parenting. The way we parent an infant should be distinctly different from how we train a toddler, how we lead an elementary student, and so on. We should see independence emerging as the child develops and gets older.

The writer of the Book of Hebrews talks about people who should be more spiritually mature but are still in an elementary mindset. It states in HEBREWS 5:12, *For when for the time ye ought to be teachers, ye have need that one teach you again which be the first principles of the oracles of God.*

It is obvious when a person is not allowed to develop on schedule.

There's a massive problem when parental involvement does not wane from first grade to high school. Coddling a child makes the child dependent and needy. This turns into toxic conditioning as the child gets older and older. When the parent is no longer in the equation, the child is left to obsess over self-preservation at the expense of his immediate community. This reality exercises the narcissistic proclivities that reside within every human being. The absolute need to rely on others for survival forces the individual into self-obsession as a survival instinct. Unknowingly, the child has been conditioned as a narcissist.

The Greatest Gift a Parent or Guardian May Give a Child Is an Intentional Responsibility for Themselves and Their Own Survival.

I had a wonderful childhood. I do not have any horror stories. For the better part of my childhood, my father was a man of significant means. He never spoiled me or my brother with luxuries. He made us work and provide for ourselves. He never coddled us. As a result, it established a mindset to grow and work for our own wants and needs. We were never allowed to believe that someone else would carry our weight. He made certain that we evolved and developed our independence on schedule.

The Apostle Paul discusses certain people in the Thessalonian Church who were leaching off the community. He says in 2 THESSALONIANS 3:10-12: *For even when we were with you, this we commanded you, that if any would not work, neither should he eat. For we hear that there are some which walk among you disorderly, working not at all, but are busybodies. Now them that are such we command and exhort by our Lord Jesus Christ, that with quietness they work, and eat their own bread.*

Paul gives us a rule for living when he said that a person should not eat anything they have not worked for. Every man must eat his own bread. When we do not demand our children or others in our community to rise to the occasion of personal responsibility, we are partakers in their stagnation.

We also have to face the fact that we sometimes indulge others because of our own needs to be needed. There are times when we paralyze our children and others because we need to be necessary. In this case, our brokenness produces another broken person.

4. ABANDONMENT

Though the list of issues that breed narcissists could continue, the final thing that we will discuss is abandonment. When a child is abandoned or is made to perceive that he is abandoned, the child, in some cases, retreats into a world of selfishness. In that child's mind, they have no one to rely on but themselves, and they must take care of their own interests above all else. Whenever we are emotionally positioned to focus primarily on ourselves, by necessity, the innate tendency for narcissistic potential is awakened.

This internal retreat is also due to the fact that the child will likely develop a deep sense of shame because of the abandonment. The child internalizes the rejection and obsesses over every conceivable reason why he must be the cause.

The PTSD (post-traumatic stress disorder) that stems from the abandonment cripples the child's sincere social skills. In other words, the child may learn to act or present a false persona to get by, to a degree, but they are never really able to sincerely belong or connect to others intimately. They never feel as though they belong and are always feeling as though they are on the outside looking in.

In their traumatized mind, they must never consider anyone else except for the purpose of using those people to supply them with what they might need. This is a twisted survival instinct.

For instance, when a kid longs for the embrace of a father or the love of a mother who never shows up, it breaks something in the soul (psyche) of that child. The actual brain of the child is negatively impacted by the trauma of rejection. It's similar to how a record is altered by a scratch. The scratch causes the record to get hung up at the point of impact.

In the case of narcissism, that childhood brokenness sometimes manifests as an angry and self-centered adult who has no capacity to sincerely consider others.

Sometimes the opposite extreme is the case—the child is self-destructive in order to please people and be accepted.

Victims of Abandonment May View It as Too Dangerous to Open Their Hearts to Let Others In.

This person does not know how to trust, how to give, or how to coexist in a healthy way with others. The person's social settings cannot move beyond self-interest for fear of more abandonment. They were limited by the scars of their childhood trauma, and their emotional stature was arrested at the point of their impact.

If this brokenness is not addressed or remedied early on in life through intense counsel, therapy, unconditional love, and acceptance, I believe that this person may be programmed into a sad state of narcissism to some lesser or greater extent. They elude connection because they have been trained to believe that no one will meet their needs.

I believe that the biblical character Cain is indirectly a great example of what a person with abandonment or rejection issues may look like in the worst-case scenario. Cain and his brother Abel brought offerings to God. Abel's offering was accepted and celebrated, while Cain's offering was rejected. God not only rejected Cain's offering; He simultaneously gave Cain instructions to re-sacrifice a more acceptable offering. Rather than following God's instructions and doing better, Cain decided to kill his brother Abel, instead.

The Bible records the story in GENESIS 4:3–8: *And in process of time it came to pass, that Cain brought of the fruit of the ground an offering unto the Lord. And Abel, he also brought of the firstlings of his flock and of the fat thereof. And the Lord had respect unto Abel and to his offering: But unto Cain and to his offering he had not respect. And Cain was very wroth, and his countenance fell. And the Lord said unto Cain, Why art thou wroth? and why is thy countenance fallen? If thou doest well, shalt thou not be accepted? and if thou doest not well, sin lieth at the door. And unto thee shall be his desire, and thou shalt rule over him. And Cain talked with Abel his brother: and it came to pass, when they were in the field, that Cain rose up against Abel his brother, and slew him.*

This story reveals a few things about the psychology of a person who perceives themselves as abandoned or rejected. Though there is no biblical evidence of Adam or Eve ever abandoning or rejecting Cain, we can clearly see that something was maladjusted in Cain's mind.

Perceived Abandonment Is as Potent as an Actual Abandonment Event.

When a person believes that they are being rejected or abandoned, it has the same effect as an actual event. The imagination is as detrimental as the actual experience.

MINDSET OF ABANDONMENT

1. They view their actions as equivalent to their value. Cain equated his worth to his performance. He clearly wanted to perform well and viewed God's correction as condemnation.

2. They are so consumed with the perceived rejection that they hear nothing apart from their own broken subconscious mind repeating, "You are not good." It is the scratched record that repeats the same message continuously.

3. They are so detached from their worth that they sometimes believe they may only improve their own position by eliminating others.

I think it's easy to conclude, even as a novice, that Cain was probably a malignant narcissist who struggled with abandonment issues for whatever reason. This is my theory as I attempt to see psychology within the framework of the Bible.

CHAPTER 3

THREE
TYPES
OF
NARCISSISTS

The study of narcissism and narcissistic personality disorder (NPD) is a very complex and opinionated subject matter. The world has given us every perspective, from trained psychiatrists, therapists, and counselors to internet therapists (people who Google and become self-ordained authorities). Regarding narcissism, we may often find certified experts who constantly contradict each other and vehemently disagree on points.

Some experts have created extensive lists of different narcissistic traits that subsequently define NPD. They are as follows: *"(1) A grand sense of self-importance; (2) fantasies about success, beauty, power, and brilliance; (3) belief that they are special and should only associate with other special people; (4) need for excessive admiration; (5) entitlement; (6) exploitative behavior; (7) lack of empathy;*

(8) envy of others and the belief that others are envious of them; and (9) an arrogant and prideful personality." This is according to the Diagnostic and Statistical Manual of Mental Disorders.

According to Experts, An Individual Would Have to Collectively Possess a Certain Number of These Traits to Be Considered a Certifiable Narcissist of Some Kind.

All Homo sapiens demonstrate these characteristics in isolation for moments. A narcissist will model multiple traits consistently.

For those who don't have the training and don't completely understand the rhetoric or the science, it may become too much to process. It's an intimidating study, to say the least. I know it has been for me. Every time you think you have it figured out; somebody has something new to add.

In my observations, **I have found it helpful to divide narcissists into three main categories: *grandiose, covert and malignant*.** These three groupings have definite lines that separate one from the others. In some cases, you can get more than one trait manifesting in a single narcissistic person. For instance, a narcissist that is fundamentally an exhibitionist (grandiose) may also manifest the aggressive tendencies of a malignant narcissist in certain situations. There may also be an occasion where a malignant narcissist may fly beneath the radar as a covert narcissist. Some have suggested that malignant narcissists move into a person's space through covert-like tactics.

Though it is common to see a blending of traits, I believe every narcissist has a dominant persona. Though the personalities and proclivities are distinctly different, it is the same diabolical spirit operating within them all. At the end of the day, it doesn't matter if your encounter was with one or the other—they all leave you confused and emotionally broken.

1. THE GRANDIOSE NARCISSIST

The grandiose narcissist has a very high need for admiration, recognition, and celebration. The exhibitionist tendencies in the grandiose narcissist resemble a little toddler who taps dances for the attention and approval of those in the room. When the toddler does not garner the attention it seeks, the toddler goes even further into a more extravagant behavior to generate approval and capture attention. This individual lives within a fantasy world where he is the supreme ruler. In his mind, he is more gifted than everyone else, and everyone else is blessed to witness his greatness.

Grandiose narcissists have very specific and unrelenting demands. They want the undivided attention of their audience. They want immediate attention. They get offended if you do not stop what you're doing to tend to their concerns. They must feel that they are perceived as the admiration of all that look on. They have the tendency to overestimate their actual importance and ability. They have a false sense of self-esteem. They buy into false illusions of their own greatness that are not substantiated by the facts of their lives. They are, on many levels, delusional. Grandiose narcissists can convince themselves that they are brilliant students even though their grades say otherwise.

The grandiose narcissist will disrupt the order of any social setting to arrest the attention and focus of the room. There's a toxic sense of entitlement that accompanies their self-delusion. They feel entitled to inconvenience others for their own selfish purposes.

You and I encounter this person more than we realize. They live in our families, work at our jobs, police our communities, run our countries and even pastor our churches.

**Grandiose Narcissists Love Positions
of Power and Prestige.**

I come from a religious context as a pastor, and I now see that I have dealt with this type of person a lot in the church. I remember a period when a certain person would consistently disturb our church services. During worship services, they would get up and walk unnecessarily in front of the congregation. This person would wait until the room was completely quiet and choose to unwrap a peppermint, or they would jostle through their bag at a serious point in the sermon. Sometimes they would not turn the ringer off on their phone, and it would make noise, drawing all attention to this individual. Every week it was something different. I am a patient man, but I was at the end of my rope.

I remember having a conversation with one of the leaders in the church about this problem. I will never forget what he said to me. He said, "She feels entitled to do whatever she wants because of who she is related to." The realization went off like a light bulb in my mind; I knew what I had been dealing with. These were definite signs of narcissistic personality disorder. This person had a complete track record of entitlement and exhibitionism. She consistently used other people for her own needs and desires. She regularly went out of her way to be seen. This was a narcissist in plain sight.

The Bible is filled with characters who would have been certifiable narcissists and many accounts of narcissism in general. One of these notable figures in the Bible is a king named Nebuchadnezzar. In fact, I believe that King Nebuchadnezzar was a type of grandiose narcissist. If you read his story, I think you'd agree. He lived with an inflated self-view. He demanded all attention be upon him, and he worshipped himself rather than The Most-High God.

The record of Nebuchadnezzar is found in DANIEL 4:28-32: *All this came upon the king Nebuchadnezzar. At the end of twelve months he walked in the palace of the kingdom of Babylon. The king spake, and said, Is not this great Babylon, that I have built for the house of the kingdom by the might of my power, and for the honour of my majesty? While the word was in the king's mouth, there fell a voice from heaven, saying, O king Nebuchadnezzar, to thee it is spoken; The kingdom is departed from thee. And they shall drive thee from men, and thy dwelling shall be with the beasts of the field: they shall make thee to eat grass as oxen, and seven times shall pass over thee, until thou know that the Most-High ruleth in the kingdom of men, and giveth it to whomsoever he will.*

Nebuchadnezzar was a grandiose narcissist. He could not recognize the sovereignty of the Most-High because he had the compulsion to put himself at center stage and claim the spotlight.

We may glean a few things from this account with Nebuchadnezzar. The first thing we see is that narcissists offend God. Even the Most-High God has a low tolerance for narcissists; you're not by yourself. The next thing we learn is that there is always a severe price to be paid for living one's life in dishonor of God and disregard for one's fellow man.

This occasion with Nebuchadnezzar is one of the accounts of a narcissist that captures their ultimate fate. If they live, they will be brought to the reality that they are not sovereign and that there is a power that transcends their delusion. The power of God humbled Nebuchadnezzar. He was brought from his grand display of pride and arrogance to crawling around in the grass like a base animal.

Narcissists Will Eventually Have to Answer for Their Actions.

Narcissists never live a full life without paying an exorbitant price for the pain they've caused. It's not for you to pay them back with the same behavior. To get even means that you must sink lower than your character should allow. All you need to do is leave them to their own devices. Every narcissist will have his own Nebuchadnezzar experience. When we don't humble ourselves, God has designed life systems to humble us. No one escapes this reality. No one.

The Bible puts it in no uncertain terms in PROVERBS 16:18–19: *Pride goeth before destruction, and an haughty spirit before a fall.* (verse 19) *Better it is to be of an humble spirit with the lowly, than to divide the spoil with the proud.*

Pride is the blinding light the grandiose narcissist stares into. Little do they know that the light they are observing is a train coming at them at full speed. If you are a Christian as I am, you may believe that there is even a judgment that goes beyond the grave. They never get away. They answer in this life or eternity.

The Grandiose Narcissist Loves Money to Reinforce His Superior Delusion.

From my personal observations, grandiose narcissists are very attracted to money and material things. When they can access an abundance of things, it reinforces their delusion of supremacy. They tend to judge success in themselves and others based on material possessions.

This idea of materialism being the standard is a reality even in Christian circles. Many feel as though one is not blessed if they don't have an abundance of things. Likewise, many feel as though their material possessions make them superior to those with less. If you ever have the misfortune of being in these people's presence, you'll notice that they spend most of their time bragging about what they have. They may be amidst a group of poor and struggling people and will go on and on about how they have more than they need. They would lack the empathy to realize how their words might be impacting the hearts of those who are not in a good place financially. They measure the quality of life by their material accumulations.

The Bible discusses the detriment of this mindset. In LUKE 12:15 it says: *And he said unto them, Take heed, and beware of covetousness: for a man's life consisteth not in the abundance of the things which he possesseth.*

What an empty soul one must have to base life upon things that can be stolen or destroyed. The grandiose narcissist has a need for these things to subsidize their twisted perspective of superiority. Their childish mind says, "I am better because mine is bigger, newer, or more expensive." What a sad existence.

2. THE COVERT NARCISSIST

Another character I want us to look at is the covert narcissist. You've heard in the movies or on television shows the phrase "covert operation." A covert operation is a secret operation that flies beneath the radar. Anything that is covert is secretive and not obvious.

A Covert Narcissist Is One Who You Would Never Suspect.

A licensed therapist named John Smith states: *"Covert narcissists appear to be very nice and helpful. They may even come off as shy and withdrawn."* Smith continues: *"Shyness is their honey trap. They appear to be the people that want to help others and are too shy to mingle. The person with low self-esteem is usually drawn into their trap. They don't possess an over the top, grandiose, outspoken opinion about how great they are, like the exhibitionist, but beneath the surface, in the back of their mind, they feel superior."* They are covert.

They are not as aggressive as the grandiose (overt) narcissist. They specialize in manipulating your personal feelings and emotions beneath the surface. The covert narcissist frequently feels belittled for no apparent reason. They tend to claim that everyone is beating up on them. They are extremely sensitive. They are the self-appointed guardians of the relational thermostat, and nobody knows the better.

Preston Ni penned an article, *"7 Signs of a Covert Introvert Narcissist,"* in Psychology Today. The covert narcissist is also known as a closet narcissist. Ni wrote, *"They demonstrate: (1) quiet smugness, (2) self-absorption, (3) lack of empathy, (4) passive aggressiveness, (5) hypersensitivity, (6) they always believe that everybody misunderstands them, and (7) they usually struggle to create healthy relationships."*

We won't have a comprehensive look at each of these symptoms of covert narcissists. However, if you ponder this list and do further research; you might be horrified at the revelations surrounding many of your relationships. The Bible describes a particular person who seems to generally fit this description in MATTHEW 7:15, where it says: *Beware of false prophets, which come to you in sheep's clothing, but inwardly they are ravening wolves.*

Covert narcissists are very dangerous, but they are undercover. They have intentionally portrayed themselves as docile and meek when the reality is that they are blood-thirsty wolves.

The psalmist said in PSALM 10:9–10, *He lieth in wait secretly as a lion in his den: he lieth in wait to catch the poor: he doth catch the poor, when he draweth him into his net. He croucheth, and humbleth himself, that the poor may fall by his strong ones.*

The covert narcissist is as stealthy as a hunting lion. He is also as lethal. There are covert narcissists camped out in all of our lives. Their impact is experienced, but rarely is the source recognized.

The Covert Narcissist Is Probably the Most Difficult to Recognize.

You might remember the fairy tale of "Little Red Riding Hood and the Big, Bad Wolf." The wolf disguised himself as Little Red Riding Hood's grandmother. He wanted to trick the little girl into falling for his trap. The wolf was engaged in a covert operation. He disguised himself to make his victim comfortable in a deadly situation.

Understanding the concept of covert narcissism should make you more dedicated to doing your due diligence in new relationships. You must ask questions and actually, listen for the answers. You must observe the motivation behind your actions. You should quietly observe the family structure and learn as much as you can about the person's childhood. Look at facial expressions along with the words being stated. You can learn a lot by paying attention and by asking questions. You never know if the person is genuine or acting when you've only had a superficial glance at the person. Go deeper.

Secrecy Is the Covert Narcissist's Weapon.

Jesus had a most polarizing disciple named Judas. His name has come to be synonymous with traitor. Judas models the secretive strategy and passive-aggressive nature of the covert narcissist. He doesn't want his target to know what he's doing. He likes to occupy the space of a friend while secretly being a jealous enemy. It was Judas who secretly arranged for Jesus' enemies to find and capture Him. Judas betrayed Jesus with a kiss.

The Bible says in MATTHEW 26:14–16, *Then one of the twelve, called Judas Iscariot, went unto the chief priests, And said unto them, What will ye give me, and I will deliver him unto you? And they covenanted with him for thirty pieces of silver. And from that time he sought opportunity to betray him.*

The covert narcissist is as dangerous as the malignant narcissist, whom we will discuss next. The covert narcissist simply disguises themselves with victimization and an image of timidity. Their attack is often more cerebral than physical. Notice the text says that Judas sought an occasion to take Jesus down. Judas plotted, and he had an agenda that was not so apparent.

The covert narcissist is incredible at playing mind games. Their specialty is knowing how to make others feel bad. They twist your world into knots and make you believe you did it to yourself.

The Covert Narcissist Creates Anxiety. Their Victim Will Experience Nervousness and Won't Always Know the Source of The Stress.

The covert narcissist creates confusion in your life, and you can't always tell where it is coming from. They have a way of tormenting your mind. They cause you to self-doubt, second-guess, accuse others, and self-condemn.

They are masters at turning the spotlight in every direction and onto every other person other than themselves.

While they create these smoke screens, they are simultaneously draining your life like a vampire would your blood. The covert narcissist manipulates every situation to blame others for their poor behavior.

There's a tale of what appears to be a helpless and pitiful character. When you listen intently to their language, it reveals what may be signs of passive-aggressive manipulation.

The Bible records this story in JOHN 5:1–9, which states: *After this there was a feast of the Jews; and Jesus went up to Jerusalem. Now there is at Jerusalem by the sheep market a pool, which is called in the Hebrew tongue Bethesda, having five porches. In these lay a great multitude of impotent folk, of blind, halt, withered, waiting for the moving of the water. For an angel went down at a certain season into the pool, and troubled the water: whosoever then first after the troubling of the water stepped in was made whole of whatsoever disease he had. And a certain man was there, which had an infirmity thirty and eight years. When Jesus saw him lie, and knew that he had been now a long time in that case, he saith unto him, Wilt thou be made whole? The impotent man answered him, Sir, I have no man, when the water is troubled, to put me into the pool: but while I am coming, another steppeth down before me. Jesus saith unto him, Rise, take up thy bed, and walk. And immediately the man was made whole, and took up his bed, and walked: and on the same day was the sabbath.*

I won't go as far as to say that this man was a narcissist because the sample size is too small to determine. We don't know enough about him. I will say that his language certainly sounds like a covert narcissist soundtrack. Covert narcissists master the language of the victim: "If only they would have, and they won't let me be great."

Notice how this man jumped at the opportunity to label himself as the victim and to blame his condition on the "unfair treatment" he had received. The reality was that he was alongside many other infirmed people. When he meets Jesus, he expresses his heart. His language, on the surface, sounds like a poor man in pain. When we look deeper, it may reveal something more diabolical.

Narcissists actually believe that they should be preferred above others. They also get very offended when they are made to play by the rules and are considered equal to others. The man from the text sounds like he felt he deserved special consideration, and his words reflect some level of offence.

His behavior and language definitely models the covert nature of those with closet narcissism. It is always cloaked in some form of injustice toward them. This softens the heart of the empath and covers up the selfish and manipulative nature of this person.

The Covert Narcissist Makes Everyone Want to Help Him While He Aims to Use Those Who Help.

"Victims want to fix their abuser while abusers want to blame their victims." —Author unknown

3. THE MALIGNANT NARCISSIST

The malignant narcissist is otherwise known as a toxic narcissist. This individual seeks to dominate others. They are very aggressive and frequently violent. They seem to take great pleasure in making others feel worthless and subjected to them like puppets. They will emotionally abuse as well as physically abuse their victims.

Some of the characteristics of the malignant narcissist are: *(1) They are quick to become aggressive and even violent, (2) they dehumanize their victims, (3) they destroy families and organizations, (4) they are generally antisocial, (5) they are sadistic, and (6) they are paranoid, just to name a few. You get the point. These are dangerous people.*

The Malignant Narcissist Is Believed
to Be the Most Dangerous.

Of all of the various subsets of narcissists, this is the one you should pray to identify sooner than later. This person can actually cost you your life.

The most famous malignant narcissist in the Bible was Jezebel. She was domineering over her husband, Ahab. She was abusive in her language, and she was sadistic in her tactics. Jezebel had no mercy for anyone, and nothing was off-limits when she was angry. Jezebel actually killed the Prophets of Jehovah.

The Bible records in 1 KINGS 18:4, *For it was so, when Jezebel cut off the prophets of the Lord, that Obadiah took an hundred prophets, and hid them by fifty in a cave, and fed them with bread and water.*

When the Bible says *cut off,* it means that she was trying to wipe them out. She would have been the female equivalent of Adolf Hitler to Jews. She was striving for the extinction of these people.

Whenever a malignant narcissist feels intimidated by another person's talents or gifts, it becomes their mission to destroy them.

Jezebel Dominated Her Husband, King Ahab.

It must have been exciting to witness that marriage. Ahab was King, but Jezebel controlled the kingdom by controlling him. I would imagine that Ahab was so subjugated he was in constant terror. The malignant narcissist gets a grip on the psyche of their victims, which forces them into an inferior posture.

The Bible says in 1 KINGS 19:1, *And Ahab told Jezebel all that Elijah had done, and withal how he had slain all the prophets with the sword.*

What's interesting is that Ahab is reporting to Jezebel even though he is the king. When you read further, you will see how Jezebel, in the king's presence, was, sending out orders. Why isn't the king giving the orders? He was married to a malignant narcissist that drained his confidence and self-respect.

Jezebel Terrorized with Her Words.

We also see how Jezebel could terrorize people with threats. Her threats were so potent because she would actually carry out the sadistic threats she would make, and everybody knew this.

Her track record is what scared the Prophet, Elijah. When she sent him a message that she would kill him, he knew that she was very capable and willing to carry this out.

The Bible says in 1 KINGS 19:2-4, *Then Jezebel sent a messenger unto Elijah, saying, So let the gods do to me, and more also, if I make not thy life as the life of one of them by tomorrow about this time. And when he saw that, he arose, and went for his life, and came to Beersheba, which belongeth to Judah, and left his servant there.*

But he himself went a day's journey into the wilderness and came and sat down under a juniper tree: and he requested for himself that he might die; and said, It is enough; now, O Lord, take away my life; for I am not better than my fathers.

Elijah was terrified of this woman because he recognized how deeply malignant, she was.

The Only Solution When Dealing with a Malignant Narcissist Is to Separate Yourself Safely and Wisely.

We will discuss strategies to disconnect from a narcissist later. When it comes to a malignant narcissist, you must put distance between yourself and them as soon as possible.

Just as Elijah ran away from Jezebel, they, too, must run from any malignant narcissist. They do not have limits, and they lack judgment. You cannot help them to change. You cannot save them. You must save yourself.

CHAPTER 4

THE
BIBLE
AND
NARCISSISM

When I first started talking about narcissism from a biblical perspective, it was amazing to some people to hear the scientific concepts expounded on from a theological vantage point. For some religious people, it was as if it were an affront to things sacred to associate the two disciplines. On the opposite side of the coin, those from the mental health community celebrated my findings.

As I studied narcissism, it was impossible for me, as a pastor, not to see its presence all through scripture. Narcissism is represented in many of the characters of the Bible, and it is described, in detail, by the Apostle Paul in his writings to his protégé Timothy. We will look at that letter extensively in this chapter.

Lucifer Is the Father of Narcissists.

Long before the existence of psychology as a science, we find the most notorious of narcissists birthed through a very powerful and popular fallen angel from Heaven. His name was Lucifer. He was very talented musically and had extremely good looks. All of these God-given qualities should have made the gifted creature grateful and humble.

Instead, Lucifer got caught up in pride and fantasies of being greater than his creator. Lucifer believed that he was greater than God.

The Bible records Lucifer's antics in ISAIAH 14:12– 14, where it says: *How art thou fallen from heaven, O Lucifer, son of the morning! how art thou cut down to the ground, which didst weaken the nations! For thou hast said in thine heart, I will ascend into heaven, I will exalt my throne above the stars of God: I will sit also upon the mount of the congregation, in the sides of the north: I will ascend above the heights of the clouds; I will be like the Most-High.*

Lucifer had become so self-indulgent he actually attempted to replace God on the throne. It wasn't enough for him to think these delusional thoughts; he actually organized a plan to overthrow the Almighty. I would say he severely overestimated his importance and power. When Lucifer had his narcissistic meltdown, God didn't take too kindly to it. God embarrassed and demoted him. God cast him down from Heaven.

JEZEBEL

We have mentioned Jezebel in the previous chapters. It's impossible to talk about narcissism within the context of the Bible and not reference Jezebel. From the information we have on Jezebel, it would probably be enough for experts to make a solid diagnosis of her having the disorder.

In the religious circles of the world, Jezebel is connected to what is called the Jezebel Spirit. This is a reference to people who are usually the equivalent of covert narcissists, who usurp the power of influential people to accomplish their own agenda and damage others. The reality concerning Jezebel is that she seemed to embody covert narcissism, malignant and grandiose, and each to a large extent.

Jezebel Is the Epitome of Narcissists.

One would be hard-pressed to find any of the narcissists in history that would surpass the sadistic nature of Jezebel. She was self-absorbed, homicidal, demanded the worship of her followers, and was as covertly deceptive as a Russian spy. Jezebel encompassed all dimensions of narcissism.

JUDAS

When I started studying and teaching about narcissism, I assumed Judas to be a narcissist. Judas was the disciple of Jesus Christ who turned him in to the Jewish authorities to be punished and eventually crucified. In my opinion, if anyone were a narcissist, it was Judas.

One day a wonderful person suggested to me that Judas could not have been a narcissist because he was so heartbroken when he learned that they were actually going to kill Jesus. He was so broken that he committed suicide. Was that a reasonable line of thought? It made me take a pause and ponder my feelings and thoughts.

Today, I'm more convinced that Judas should be included in what I call the Biblical Narcissist Hall of Shame.

Just Because a Person Demonstrates Remorse Does Not Disqualify Them from Being a Narcissist.

Judas could have been remorseful for several self-serving reasons. When he realized they were going to kill Jesus, it meant that he would subsequently lose his status. He was connected to the most powerful and popular man in Israel. He was the treasurer of Jesus' ministry. When Judas realized they were going to kill Jesus, he also knew that the other disciples would eventually kill him. Judas also had to know that Jesus' massive followers would hate him.

In my opinion, it's not enough to conclude that Judas wasn't a narcissist because he demonstrated remorse. He may have very well been sorry, but he was sorry for the personal consequences of a poorly executed, covert scheme.

We can see the signs in Judas from the biblical record.

The Bible says in MATTHEW 26:7–16, *There came unto him a woman having an alabaster box of very precious ointment, and poured it on his head, as he sat at meat. But when his disciples saw it, they had indignation, saying, to what purpose is this waste? For this ointment might have been sold for much, and given to the poor. When Jesus understood it, he said unto them, Why trouble ye the woman? for she hath wrought a good work upon me. For ye have the poor always with you; but me ye have not always. For in that she hath poured this ointment on my body, she did it for my burial. Verily I say unto you, wheresoever this gospel shall be preached in the whole world, there shall also this, that this woman hath done, be told for a memorial of her.*

Then one of the twelve, called Judas Iscariot, went unto the chief priests, And said unto them, What will ye give me, and I will deliver him unto you? And they covenanted with him for thirty pieces of silver. And from that time he sought opportunity to betray him.

From this biblical text, we can see that Judas' motivation for betrayal was clearly jealousy. He got upset when he realized the cost of the ointment the woman gave to Jesus. This is a classic sign of narcissism. He felt like this should have been done for him. We also see how Judas created a covert plot to betray Jesus starting from that point. He even cut a deal with Jesus' enemies. I think that there is more evidence proving Judas is a narcissist than not. You decide for yourself.

In another record of the same story, found in JOHN 12:4-5, Judas uses passive-aggressive tactics to make Jesus feel bad for accepting the precious oil. It says: *Then saith one of his disciples, Judas Iscariot, Simon's son, which should betray him, Why was not this ointment sold for three hundred pence, and given to the poor?*

I personally think he was a narcissist. A classic maneuver of a narcissist is to twist the things others should feel good about into something shameful and bad. They are the masters of raining on every parade.

THE APOSTLE PAUL'S DESCRIPTION OF NARCISSISM IN THE CHURCH LEADERSHIP

With all of the many narcissistic characters in the Bible, there is a greater biblical reference supporting the connection between the disorder and the Bible. The Apostle Paul outlines in detail the characteristics of a generation of leaders for Timothy, a young pastor, to be aware of. This was a self-centered, self-absorbed, and self-serving people. His language in this letter sounds like a doctoral student's thesis on narcissistic characteristics.

It is found in 2 TIMOTHY 3:1-7, *This know also, that in the last days perilous times shall come. For men shall be lovers of their own selves, covetous, boasters, proud, blasphemers, disobedient to parents, unthankful, unholy, Without natural affection, trucebreakers, false accusers, incontinent, fierce, despisers of those that are good, Traitors, heady, high-minded, lovers of pleasures more than lovers of God; Having a form of godliness, but denying the power thereof: from such turn away. For of this sort are they which creep into houses, and lead captive silly women laden with sins, led away with divers lusts, Ever learning, and never able to come to the knowledge of the truth.*

The Apostle is describing a group of people who are unruly, unteachable, and overall toxic to the Christian community. He's making the young and inexperienced pastors aware of their presence and their tactics.

Paul outlines nineteen characteristics that directly relate to the profile of any narcissist. Eleven are described here.

LOVERS OF THEMSELVES

Paul starts the list with the fact that these people are lovers of themselves. A narcissist is in love with one person, and that person is himself. The very concept is taken from the Greek mythological figure Narcissus, the man who gazed upon his own image in the water and fell madly in love with himself.

Some psychologists suggest to us that at the core of the narcissist's dysfunctional perspective is either a childhood where they were deprived of love and attention or one where they were immersed in an overdose of adoration and attention by a doting parent or caregiver. This amounts to the narcissist feeling an obsession with self-adoration to compensate for the lack of it, or they are simply perpetuating the fallacy of being the center of the universe. In either case, they are programmed to love themselves and not another.

Paul describes this generation of toxic Christians as self-lovers.

COVETOUS

Paul also described these people as covetous. To covet means to have an intense desire for what belongs to another person. Narcissists are covetous of other people's possessions, influence, physical features, relationships, and power.

This is an obsession with other people and the things they believe should rightfully be theirs.

The Bible says in JAMES 4:2, *You desire and do not have, so you murder. You covet and cannot obtain, so you fight and quarrel. You do not have, because you do not ask.*

The message of this particular text is reminiscent of Lucifer and his coveting of the Almighty's throne and power.

A Narcissist Lives with the Lie That They Are the Greatest. When Someone Possesses Something The Narcissist Doesn't Have, It Contradicts Their False Identity and Feels Like an Injury.

There is such a thing as a narcissistic injury. A narcissistic injury hurts the structure of the narcissist's false self. It is anything that brings them face to face with the reality that they are not what they've imagined.

When someone outshines the narcissist in any way, it creates an injury. From that moment, that person becomes enemy number one, and they strive to supplant that person's greatness. Most of the time, the person does not realize they are in a competition.

When I was younger, I had a very bad habit of surrounding myself with people who needed me but didn't deserve me. Consequently, I took on a team of various types of narcissists. My mother and my wife would try to warn me, but I always felt like I could change these narcissists.

When I started to pay attention, I realized there was this obsession with everything I did or had in some of them. It was scary. This was more than a person that admires another; this was a competition I had not realized I was participating in. It started to feel very demonic. Today I know the difference between admiration and covetousness.

BOASTERS

This is so plainly descriptive of the narcissist. If narcissists are nothing else, they are boastful. They are delusional and blind to reality. The narcissist has conjured a preferred reality as opposed to what actually is. They brag about their accomplishments and finances like they are bursting with success when the actual facts dictate that they are in bankruptcy. Narcissists are very elaborate liars as well.

The narcissist can take a small pebble and use conjecture to recreate it into a mountain. They can take a minimum wage job and describe it as paying six figures and including a company car. They have a need to make themselves bigger. Narcissist has the imagination and propensity to embellish like a first-grade student, and they need everyone to know how great they are and how much they have.

It says in JAMES 4:13–16, *Come now, you who say, "Today or tomorrow we will go into such and such a town and spend a year there and trade and make a profit"—yet you do not know what tomorrow will bring. What is your life? For you are a mist that appears for a little time and then vanishes. Instead you ought to say, "If the Lord wills, we will live and do this or that." As it is, you boast in your arrogance. All such boasting is evil.*

The narcissist boasts as if he is a god and in sovereign control of all things. The Bible calls this evil. Have you ever wondered why certain people that go on and on about their "accomplishments" and greatness tend to irritate you? There's a spirit behind this bragging that is more than someone being excited about their advancement. This is a spirit that desires to self-promote while belittling others.

PROUD

Everyone should have a healthy pride about themselves and their accomplishments. However, the narcissist has a toxic pride that makes them impossible to coexist with.

Everyone Who Has Self-Pride Is Not Necessarily a Narcissist.

Narcissistic pride is condescending and abusive. This is the kind of self-exaltation that even gets a negative reaction out of God.

There are six things that Proverbs declares God hates. The first on the list is a proud look. It's such a narcissistic pride that it shows, even on the countenance of the person.

Have you ever looked at a person and could actually see the sickness of their soul plastered on their face like a mask?

The Bible says in PROVERBS 6:16–17, *These six things doth the Lord hate: yea, seven are an abomination unto him: A proud look, a lying tongue, and hands that shed innocent blood.*

A proud look is the first he mentions. The pride of a narcissist is very intense. Every conversation has to be centered around them. They are entirely concerned about the way they look. They would miss their mother's funeral if they didn't have the right dress. They would exhibit an arrogant attitude toward Mother Teresa. The narcissist has a need for everyone else to diminish so that they may feel superior. There is no such thing as a compromise; it must always go the way they want it to go. They do not sense anyone's need but their own.

Their Narcissistic Pride Destroys Any Healthy Relationship. They Can't Maintain Romances or Friendships.

The Bible says in DANIEL 5:18–20, *O thou king, the most high God gave Nebuchadnezzar thy father a kingdom, and majesty, and glory, and honour: And for the majesty that he gave him, all people, nations, and languages, trembled and feared before him: whom he would he slew; and whom he would he kept alive; and whom he would he set up; and whom he would he put down. But when his heart was lifted up, and his mind hardened in pride, he was deposed from his kingly throne, and they took his glory from him.*

The reason Daniel was reminding Belshazzar of his father's history is because Belshazzar was walking with the same pride and arrogance that got his father deposed by the Almighty God. Narcissists really do produce narcissists.

DISOBEDIENT TO PARENTS

This is an interesting description that Paul uses. He says to Timothy that narcissists will be disobedient to their parents. It's interesting because most psychologists agree that narcissists are created through poor parental experiences.

As a consequence, the principles of authority and leadership are not conceivable within the mind of the narcissist.

Narcissists Are Often Rebellious to All Authority.

Parental authority is where we learn to respect and adhere to society's various dimensions of authority. Narcissists have no respect for any authority. They are blatantly rebellious, or they exercise a passive rebellion. This is also symbolic of the spirit of Lucifer.

The wisdom of PROVERBS 17:11 says: *An evil man seeks only rebellion, and a cruel messenger will be sent against him.*

Narcissists do not have the heart to comply or to submit. The result is always a consequence that is brutal and unnecessary. This is why they end up in prison, and often they are killed. They are rebellious by nature.

UNTHANKFUL

The narcissist is deficient in gratitude. One may slit his wrist and bleed for the narcissist and never get a thank you. They are so empty they don't even recognize the moments they should be grateful.

There Is Always Something More the Narcissist Believes You Should Do for Them.

Have you ever known a person that you nearly break yourself for, and they look at you as if you've done nothing? The insanity of the entire relationship is that they somehow make you believe that you should do more and that the problem is in your lack of generosity.

You Cannot Do Anything to Please an Ingrate!

The Bible says in ROMANS 1:21, *For although they knew God, they did not honor him as God or give thanks to him, but they became futile in their thinking, and their foolish hearts were darkened.*

The ungrateful and unthankful person becomes worse, not better. Their hearts become darkened. They lack the capacity to see the benefits before them.

A Narcissist Will Not Appreciate a Great Relationship Until He Destroys It. After It's Destroyed, He Will Long for the Benefit It Once Provided, Not the Person.

TRUCE BREAKERS

A truce breaker, by definition, is one who fails to honor a covenant. A narcissist is incapable of fulfilling any covenant that requires them to consider the other's feelings or needs. When a narcissist feels the need to take advantage or violate an agreement, it is as good as done. By nature, they are committed to no one but themselves.

The Bible looks negatively upon people who do not keep their vows. The Bible declares that God is a covenant-keeping God.

The word of God says in NUMBERS 30:1-2, *Moses spoke to the heads of the tribes of the people of Israel, saying, "This is what the Lord has commanded. If a man vows a vow to the Lord, or swears an oath to bind himself by a pledge, he shall not break his word. He shall do according to all that proceeds out of his mouth."*

What God is calling for in this passage is the antithesis of a narcissist. A narcissist will usually do the exact opposite of what they vowed to do. The narcissist is a liar by nature. There can be no respect for any covenant in the life of a narcissist because there is no truth in them.

Jesus describes Satan in JOHN 8:44, and he says, *Ye are of your father the devil, and the lusts of your father ye will do. He was a murderer from the beginning, and abode not in the truth, because there is no truth in him. When he speaketh a lie, he speaketh of his own: for he is a liar, and the father of it.*

I believe that Satan is the father of narcissists. A narcissist will produce the same fruit of the root they are spawn from. Lucifer was a truce breaker.

FALSE ACCUSERS

The Apostle Paul went further in 2 TIMOTHY 3 to describe narcissists as false accusers. This speaks for itself. These people will lie about anybody. They will make up a narrative that puts them in a favorable light. It does not matter if the lie destroys a person's career, reputation, and/or family; they will bring up accusations against anybody.

The Bible continuously stands against bearing false witness against others. The Bible directly instructs in

EXODUS 23:1, *You shall not spread a false report. You shall not join hands with a wicked man to be a malicious witness.*

Narcissists Thrive on False Reports. It's One of the Ways They Destroy Their Victim's Credibility in the Community.

DESPISERS OF THOSE WHO ARE GOOD

The narcissist has a disdain for people who are actually authentically good. They despise those who are morally good. They hate those who are good at whatever they do. They despise anything good.

When a Narcissist Sees an Authentically Good Person, It Is Viewed as a Reflection of Themselves and Their Shortcomings.

When narcissist witnesses another person's good deeds or character, they simultaneously feel as though the spotlight is instantly on their flaws. They become anxious and offended because there's no context where they are not at the center of any moment. In their minds, the world can't perceive you without simultaneously seeing them. When a narcissist feels they don't measure up to another person, they may work to destroy them.

There's a record of King Saul trying to kill David, who had done nothing but serve him. It is found in 1 SAMUEL 18:6–11, *And it came to pass as they came, when David was returned from the slaughter of the Philistine, that the women came out of all cities of Israel, singing and dancing, to meet king Saul, with tabrets, with joy, and with instruments of musick. And the women answered one another as they played, and said, Saul hath slain his thousands, and David his ten thousands. And Saul was very wroth, and the saying displeased him; and he said, They have ascribed unto David ten thousands, and to me they have ascribed but thousands: and what can he have more but the kingdom? And Saul eyed David from that day and forward.*

And it came to pass on the morrow, that the evil spirit from God came upon Saul, and he prophesied in the midst of the house: and David played with his hand, as at other times: and there was a javelin in Saul's hand. And Saul cast the javelin; for he said, I will smite David even to the wall with it. And David avoided out of his presence twice.

David was only guilty of fighting Saul's battles and expanding Saul's kingdom, and Saul literally wanted to murder him.

All You Need Do to Invoke the Rage of a Malignant Narcissist Is Be Good.

LOVERS OF PLEASURES

The empty self-esteem bank of narcissists makes them place a high value on extracurricular activities. They like to portray themselves as having a successful life through activities and possessions.

The Narcissist Uses Pleasure to Subsidize the Emptiness of Their Life.

Many narcissists love material things. Buying and displaying make them happy. They define themselves and their success based on their access to luxury and exclusive material trappings.

The problem with this happiness they've concocted is that it is short-lived, and they are continuously in pursuit of this pleasure.

Some psychologists refer to this as the hedonic treadmill. The hedonic treadmill is based on a person's ambitions to achieve more or to have more to make one happier, only to discover that none of it results in a happier state. They are on a treadmill that wears them out but goes nowhere. More money, more food, and more wine often end in greater misery.

There's a parable that Jesus shared with his disciples about a rich man who placed all of his efforts into having more. The man's superficial response to Jesus was sad.

The Bible says in LUKE 12:18–21, *And he said, This will I do: I will pull down my barns, and build greater; and there will I bestow all my fruits and my goods. And I will say to my soul, Soul, thou hast much goods laid up for many years;*

take thine ease, eat, drink, and be merry. But God said unto him, Thou fool, this night thy soul shall be required of thee: then whose shall those things be, which thou hast provided? So is he that layeth up treasure for himself, and is not rich toward God.

A narcissist is rich in the things that are irrelevant and impoverished with eternal things.

HAVING A FORM OF GODLINESS

The final attribute we will look at in Paul's list is "a form of godliness." Contrary to popular opinion, narcissists are heavily involved in things religious. Religion provides a wonderful backdrop for their feelings of superiority to be played out in self-righteousness. Religion justifies their assault on the self-esteem of weaker victims.

Narcissists Are Religious, but They Are Not Spiritual. They Use Religion, but They Have No Relationship with God.

When we read the gospels, we see the Pharisees and the Sadducees. These men were the religious leaders of Israel and Jews; most of them were narcissists. They only had a form of godliness. Their relationship with God ended with their traditions and rituals. In many cases, there were no deep, authentic spiritual encounters.

Religions, of Every Brand, Have Always Attracted Spiritual Narcissists.

A spiritual narcissist uses the pretense of religious piety to manipulate others. Throughout history, you'll find narcissists at the helm of every religion at some point in time.

People have witnessed too many who have had a form of godliness without any real conviction. These amounts to narcissistic opportunists who use the platform of the church to preach self-worship and to establish cults rather than holy spaces.

CHAPTER 5

THE IMPACT OF NARCISSISTIC ABUSE

I was blindsided by the reality of narcissistic abuse. I had viewed narcissism as simply the inconvenience of having to share space with an obnoxious, egotistic, self-promoting jerk. I didn't realize what I was in for when the full scope of this issue was revealed to me.

I think it was around 2018 when I started studying and discussing narcissism on social media and even in the churches I pastored. Occasionally, I would travel and discuss the issue at conferences. I never presented myself as an expert. I was always clear that my findings were those of a neophyte, as I was new to the study and had no real scientific skill in helping others to process such a situation.

It was amazing how people were reaching out from around the world and responding to my message. It was exciting to resonate with so many thousands of diverse people.

Then it hit me like a ton of bricks! My email inbox, airport chats, and conversations in book-signing lines at my conferences began to reveal how utterly destroyed many of these victims of narcissistic abuse were. Some were on the brink of suicide. Others had become socially dysfunctional. The depression and anxiety were so great they couldn't work jobs or continue their careers. Their nerves were so on edge that many looked decades older than their identification dictated. This was more serious than I had realized.

I started to understand that a narcissist's impact on a victim's life is not some surface-level annoyance, like a fly buzzing about the ear; this was more like a snake attached to the main artery and constantly pumping venom. This was a matter of life or death.

The Narcissist Is Hunting for the Soul of the Victim.

Almost daily, I am embraced by someone struggling to get back to their life because of narcissistic abuse. The most hurtful aspect of their horrifying experience is that very few people can conceive of such diabolical, underhanded shenanigans. The narcissist can destroy a person in plain sight, and no one would be the wiser. Normal people cannot imagine the things a narcissist does to drain their victim's soul.

As I have begun to understand the fringes of this issue, I am compelled to describe it as purely demonic. No one human being is capable of the actions and schemes to injure another person like narcissists are. The concepts of ghosting, gaslighting, or hoovering are spiritual in nature, and there's nothing holy about it. These thoughts do not emanate from a human soul alone, and certainly, God does not author such confusion. This is the work of demons.

There are signs that one is suffering from narcissistic abuse. Narcissistic abuse syndrome is simply the emotional and physiological impact the behavior of a narcissist has on the victim.

I Believe That Narcissistic Abuse May Damage the Brain.

Kim Saeed, author, researcher, and educator, in her blog titled "Long-Term Narcissistic Abuse Can Cause Brain Damage," says: "...*repeated emotional trauma leads to both PTSD and C-PTSD, which should be reason enough to leave an abusive partner. But, what many people don't realize is that over time, these repeated emotional injuries shrink the hippocampus, which is responsible for memory and learning, while enlarging the amygdala, which houses primitive emotions such as fear, grief, guilt, envy and shame.*"

There are certain predictable outcomes when a person engages a narcissist in a close relationship. In some circles, this is labeled as narcissistic victim syndrome.

THE VICTIM CHECKS OUT ON LIFE AND DETACHES FROM WHAT ONCE MATTERED

One of the primary signs of a person who may be under the stress of narcissistic abuse is when they begin to disconnect from the life they created. They were always at the club or in the church, and now they are nowhere to be found. They valued education, and now there's no passion. They are by nature someone who is meticulous about their appearance, and now they couldn't care less.

When you, as an individual, are dealing with narcissistic abuse syndrome, you feel emotionally or even physically detached from your world. You lose your sense of self and who you are. You forget what truly matters, and you find it difficult to make a decision.

**The Official Term Used to Define
This State Is Dissociation.**

Dissociation is a psychological experience in which people feel disconnected from their thought processes, their sense of self, or personal values. When a narcissist does their diabolical work on a person's soul, they are disconnected from themselves and everything else. They are functionally a psychological zombie. It's so bad that they appear to be under the influence of some substance.

The Traumatized Person Is So Confused About Their Existence That Their Mind Checks Out.

The Bible describes a state of existence in 1 TIMOTHY 4:1–2, where it says: *Now the Spirit speaketh expressly, that in the latter times some shall depart from the faith, giving heed to seducing spirits, and doctrines of devils; Speaking lies in hypocrisy; having their conscience seared with a hot iron.*

The Apostle Paul raises a very troubling issue when he says they give heed to seducing spirits. A seducing spirit is an impostor that circumvents a person's defenses and lodges in the individual's mind to control their choices and feelings. You'll also notice that the verse says their conscience will be seared with a hot iron. This speaks of separating the person from their sense of right versus wrong. The description of a hot iron searing the senses is similar to a person burning their fingers on a stove. The senses would be so damaged that the person would probably have no sensation for a while, if ever again. When a person has been traumatized by a seducing spirit, they are desensitized.

THE VICTIM WILL OFTEN LIVE AS A PEOPLE PLEASER

The fear of creating a backlash makes the victim hyper-sensitive to the wishes of others. They do not want to do anything to set off an episode. They have been made so fearful of the abuser that they are living in a prison of anxiety. They would rather humiliate themselves than to reap the backlash of their victimizer.

The Bible describes this heightened anxiety in PROVERBS 29:25–26: *The fear of man bringeth a snare: but whoso putteth his trust in the Lord shall be safe. Many seek the ruler's favour; but every man's judgment cometh from the Lord.*

The snare is a trap. Narcissistic abuse establishes a trap for the soul. Narcissistic abuse positions the abuser as god. You'll find yourself living to please him.

The extended fallout is when your people-pleasing habits begin to apply to the entire world. You forget how to have an opinion or position, and now you live your entire life seeking to please everyone you encounter. The soul is broken, and you can no longer engage your individuality.

THE VICTIM BEGINS TO SACRIFICE ALL OF THEIR PERSONAL NEEDS TO ACCOMMODATE THE ABUSER

When a person is deep into narcissistic abuse, they will deplete themselves of things necessary to please the abuser. It's not uncommon for a victim to bankrupt themselves for a narcissist. You live to meet the other person's needs and desires, even when they are disrespectful and hurtful.

I remember I was attending a conference. At the end of the conference, a dear lady walked up to me and shared that she was housing an adult son who was unemployed and disrespectful to her. I asked her: "So you're telling me that this man is grown, unemployed by choice, lives in your house, and disrespects you?" She said, "Yes, sir." I had to pause and choose my words carefully because I realized that I was dealing with a traumatized psyche. These were the words of a person who a malignant narcissist had emotionally subjugated, and it happened to be her own child. As we progressed in the conversation, she said to me: "My children are all I have." I understand that concept, having four children of my own; however, disrespect and enablement are not on the agenda

A Narcissist Will Use You to Any Extent.

In ACTS 16:16-19, we find a record of a woman who was being used by a band of narcissists. It says: *And it came to pass, as we went to prayer, a certain damsel possessed with a spirit of divination met us, which brought her masters much gain by soothsaying: The same followed Paul and us, and cried, saying, These men are the servants of the most high God, which shew unto us the way of salvation. And this did she many days. But Paul, being grieved, turned and said to the spirit, I command thee in the name of Jesus Christ to come out of her. And he came out the same hour. And when her masters saw that the hope of their gains was gone, they caught Paul and Silas, and drew them into the marketplace unto the rulers.*

Pay attention to the latter part, when they saw that hope of their gains was gone, and they took action. They used this poor woman, and she lived to be used by them. Also, note that the woman had been possessed by a demonic spirit. One of the things I truly believe as a spiritual person is that narcissists are demonically empowered. Just like these men had no shame or limits in terms of using this woman, a narcissist will drain a victim of everything. And just like the lady in the text, you'll give more than you can afford to please the narcissist's demands.

VICTIMS FIND IT EXTREMELY CHALLENGING TO TRUST

The individual who has endured narcissistic abuse becomes paranoid in the midst of people and about the proposition of relationships. I have met people who were victims of narcissistic abuse, and they could barely look me in the eye. Some were very shy about even having a conversation.

When the victim is in the midst of a relationship with the narcissist, this distrust is based on the abuser's manipulation and control over the victim's social life.

The Narcissist Can Make a Victim Distrust Their Own Mother.

An even greater impact of distrust is experienced after the relationship has ended. When a person has miraculously escaped the snares of a narcissist, it leaves them so broken that they don't want to risk being vulnerable again.

There's a phobia of people that overwhelms the victim of narcissistic abuse. They'd rather spend their lives alone than take the chance of being caught up again in another narcissistic trap. The victim puts walls around their heart because of terror.

The Bible says in PROVERBS 18:19, *A brother offended is harder to be won than a strong city: and their contentions are like the bars of a castle.*

We could paraphrase this verse: A person who has been burned will not be convinced to warm by the fire. When a person has been hurt, they establish hard boundaries around themselves that others will find impossible to penetrate. This is a common result of narcissistic abuse.

VICTIMS MAY DEVELOP A DESIRE TO END THEIR LIVES

It is just this serious. Victims of extreme narcissistic abuse quite often have fantasies about suicide. Their lives have been so devastated that they view death as a better alternative to living. The irony in that thought demonstrates how diabolical this entire dynamic is.

I have had to talk many people out of the idea of ending their lives. Somehow you must bring them back to their reasons for living and the people who need them. They have dissociated to the point where they cannot see anything but death as a viable option.

Dr. Richard McKeon, chief of the suicide prevention branch at the US Substance Abuse and Mental Health Services Administration, notes that victims of intimate partner violence are twice as likely to attempt suicide multiple times. This is the way abusers essentially commit murder without a trace.

These narcissists are as stealthy as a poisonous gas in their dealings. When their antics have had the full effect, it leaves a person so crushed they may not want to be alive anymore. This was the case with Elijah in his encounter with Jezebel. When Jezebel sent a message to Elijah, the spirit of the message impacted him in such a way that it led him to pray for death.

The Bible records the story in 1 KINGS 19:1–5. It says: *Now Ahab told Jezebel all that Elijah had done, and how he had killed all the prophets [of Baal] with the sword. Then Jezebel sent a messenger to Elijah, saying, "So may the gods do to me, and even more, if by this time tomorrow I do not make your life like the life of one of them." And Elijah was afraid and arose and ran for his life, and he came to Beersheba which belongs to Judah, and he left his servant there. But he himself traveled a day's journey into the wilderness, and he came and sat down under a juniper tree and asked [God] that he might die. He said, "It is enough; now, O Lord, take my life, for I am no better than my fathers." He lay down and slept under the juniper tree, and behold, an angel touched him and said to him, "Get up and eat."*

Elijah prayed to die. Elijah ran for his life. He secluded himself in a cave, and he used self-destructive language. God had to come to him to have a calm conversation and to refocus Elijah on his purpose.

These are keys to helping a person suffering from narcissistic abuse that may want to die. They don't need harsh judgment. They need intentional conversation and to be refocused on life. Never say, "Snap out of it."

VICTIMS ARE IMPRISONED BY COMPARISONS

A major part of narcissistic abuse is to break down the victim's self-perspective. One of the narcissist's major weapons in this endeavor is to draw comparisons between the victim and another person. The comparison will always make the other person superior to the victim.

For instance, a man who is abusing a woman will compare her body or features to another woman who is the total opposite of her. This is to put her in an impossible race to become something she can never be. A woman will do the same thing to a male victim. She will compare her former millionaire boyfriend's choices of restaurant to the kind her present boyfriend can afford.

These tactics are to bring the victim into a state of mind where they internalize the fear that they are not enough. This consumes the victim's psyche proving that they are at least equal.

Narcissistic Abuse Victims Spend Their Lives Competing for Acceptance and Approval.

The Bible states in GALATIANS 1:10 in the Amplified version: *Am I now trying to win the favor and approval of men, or of God? Or am I seeking to please someone? If I were still trying to be popular with men, I would not be a bond-servant of Christ.*

The Apostle Paul clarifies that we must live our lives to please the Creator and never men. When you compete with people for someone's approval, you should recognize that you are being victimized emotionally.

This is one of the classic games womanizers play. They will draw comparisons between two women to break the self-confidence of one of them. The comparison plants a seed of low value in the woman's mind and creates a ferocious desire to be accepted by the person who made her feel inadequate. The woman will do practically anything to win the approval of that particular man. She fails to understand that he will never give her that approval. The intent was always to get her addicted to his approval, and he used the bait of comparison to accomplish it. This is one of the narcissist's chief strategies.

VICTIMS SOMETIMES DEFEND THEIR ABUSERS

Victims of narcissistic abuse will find ways to make the abuse their fault. The trauma bond between them and the abuser keeps them hopeful that the abuser will change or that somehow it would not have happened if they had been a better friend, spouse, or partner. The broken consciousness rushes to take the blame.

Another reason why victims self-blame is because they want to defend the reputation of the offender to their circle and the people who matter to them. Sometimes they've been so emotionally traumatized that they actually believe that they caused the physical and verbal abuse and don't want their family and friends to think poorly of their victimizer. They don't see themselves as victims yet. They view themselves as deserving of the treatment they are getting. In some sick way, they may view the abuser as the victim.

Victims may protect their abusers from legal consequences by refusing to press charges or refusing to call the
authorities.

This is a severe problem in certain religious environments where people are taught to fight for their relationships. People are made to believe that God gave this
person to them. Though the individual is threatening their
lives and violent, religious fanatics insist that it is "God's
will" for the victims to fight for their relationship.

When the relationship falls apart, the victims are
challenged with ideas of spiritual failure. In their minds,
they have not experienced a bad relationship—they have
disappointed God, and they have embarrassed the church.

Rather than admit that they are being abused by this
"God-sent man," they cover it up, make excuses, and will
ultimately take the blame for the dysfunction in the union
before they admit they were deceived and made a mistake
that God had nothing to do with it. They tell themselves
this lie so much that they believe it themselves. They
believe that they are the problem.

There's a story in the Bible about a man named Jacob
who had two wives—one he loved (Rachel) and the other
he hated (Leah). There's no indication of Jacob physically
abusing Leah, but he definitely abused her emotionally. He
never wanted to marry her, but he was forced.

There's an interesting account of her mental state
under the pressure of this abuse. She made excuses and
blamed the poor treatment she received from him on her
failure to perform.

The record of this story is found in GENESIS 29:31–
35. It states: *And when the Lord saw that Leah was hated,*

he opened her womb: but Rachel was barren. And Leah conceived, and bare a son, and she called his name Reuben: for she said, Surely the Lord hath looked upon my affliction; now therefore my husband will love me. And she conceived again, and bare a son; and said, Because the Lord hath heard that I was hated, he hath therefore given me this son also: and she called his name Simeon. And she conceived again, and bare a son; and said, Now this time will my husband be joined unto me, because I have born him three sons: therefore was his name called Levi. And she conceived again, and bare a son: and she said, Now will I praise the Lord: therefore she called his name Judah; and left bearing.

When you read this story, you will discern a woman with a broken consciousness. She was living for approval, and she internalized the lack of love she received to the point where she took responsibility for his dysfunction. Notice how she kept trying to perform her way into acceptance. What prevented her from seeing that this man was toxic and abusive? She kept believing that another baby would solve the problem. Her mind told her that she was the root and had to fix it.

The thing all of us must realize is that narcissists exist at every level of a relationship. They are in our schools and even in our jobs. They are the masters of twisting the minds of others into a pretzel. They will offend you on the job and twist it in a way that makes you feel bad for confronting them for an obvious violation.

It Is Imperative That We All Think About the Spirit Behind All of Our Relationships, Lest We Be Victims Unaware.

When you have a good and giving heart, narcissists will find a way to capitalize on you. As a pastor, I have encountered this spirit many times. I've been made to feel that certain things were my fault. When I really stepped away from the moment and thought it through, I realized a narcissistic spirit was manipulating me. Sometimes I confronted the person, and other times I simply moved on with awareness. All of us, to some degree, lesser or greater, are impacted by narcissistic abuse.

CHAPTER 6

MARRIED TO
A
NARCISSIST

I remember many years ago, I had a marital counseling session with a couple. The wife seemed hysterical and irrational. She seemed like she was off of her rocker or on drugs of some kind. The irony was she was the one that pleaded for the session. The husband seemed calm and rational. He didn't understand the need for counseling, but he submitted to her wishes. She made outlandish accusations of him that seemed unfounded and overly dramatic.

I must admit, based on my initial impression of her, I had a definite sense of prejudice; I prejudged the lady as probably being the problem. This was because of preconceived impressions that were based on their polar opposite dispositions. She seemed unsettled, while he seemed stable.

As the session continued and I began to probe gently for the facts and the unspoken realities, I started to see that this lady was emotionally confused because her partner was manipulating the optics. He was making her appear to be the unstable woman and himself appear as the pillar of stability and the rational husband. As I went deeper, I discovered that this lady was really a victim of emotional abuse.

At the time, I did not have the language to describe or define what I witnessed. I was witnessing a wife who was under the pressure of narcissistic abuse. She was in a marriage with a narcissist. As I unpacked the facts of their situation, I observed a very diabolical personality behind the mask of this pseudo-upstanding gentleman. I asked questions that broke through the façade he had created, and he became most uncomfortable, even angry. There were some questions that he avoided altogether. He went from being a calm, dignified gentleman to an unpredictable, visibly upset controller.

MARRIED TO A NARCISSIST

Being married to a narcissist is like being married to a vampire. Narcissists survive by draining the life of their spouses (victims). They don't only drain the life of their spouse; they drain the life of their children and everyone else closely involved.

As a child, I spent much time with certain relatives. I always knew that something was not altogether right with the husband. He had an uncanny gift for negatively controlling the atmosphere in the room and dictating everyone's mood.

He constantly berated his wife, who only lived to serve him. He criticized his grown children and, at times would become physical with the grandchildren of the family. This guy, in my opinion, was a malignant narcissist. He drained the energy out of the entire family— his wife, his children, and even his grandchildren. This guy was my maternal grandfather.

I must take this opportunity to make a very serious point. Though I was present to witness this bizarre and dysfunctional behavior as a child, I knew it wasn't right. I believe that the health of my own parents' relationship shielded my soul from the infection of narcissistic contact. What's more is that I knew enough to realize that his behavior was abusive, and yet, I could still love him within healthy boundaries. It's as if I knew who he was, understood his tactics, and was never impacted because of the healthy values I experienced at my own house. Parenting is extremely important.

I didn't know what I was witnessing at the time, but I knew it was toxic, it wasn't normal, and it wasn't right. I watched my grandmother exist in a relationship where she was constantly criticized, called out of her name, and never celebrated by a man that she slaved for.

She worked as a domestic. She would work a full day's work, and then she would come home to cook, clean, and cater to my grandfather—and he seemed to live to destroy her confidence.

My grandmother was a classic empath. She took care of everyone's issues. My grandfather felt entitled to be catered to. He even seemed to expect worship. My grandmother was married to a narcissist. The consequence was we were all married to a narcissist.

Marriage Is Ideally Supposed to Be a Mutually Beneficial Enterprise. When One Is Joined to a Narcissist, It Is a One-Way Street.

A narcissist is constantly positioning their spouse to be taken advantage of. They are in the marriage solely for what they can extract. They are not present to make a deposit. They walk around with a fistful of withdrawal slips, while their partners usually carry all of the deposit slips.

In general, I have observed that a narcissistic wife will manipulate her husband's natural desire to provide and protect. This lady will buy things and create enormous debt and watch him struggle to pay for this unnecessary and wasteful indulgence. He is conditioned to serve the desires of his wife. If he doesn't, he's made to feel like he's less of a man. He's controlled through false impressions of guilt and inadequacy. He rarely sees his wife as the demonic user she actually is, and no one can tell him differently.

The narcissistic husband usually plays on the wife's natural empathy and her desire to serve her family. He uses this sacred and pure heart to reposition her as a modern slave. She won't be able to locate an identity apart from being one who serves her demonic dictator.

The Narcissistic Spouse Serves to Take the Power, Will, and Identity from Their Partner. The Aim Is to Make Them into a Puppet.

We may observe some of this, beneath the surface, in the relationship between King Ahab and his wife, Jezebel. Jezebel completely and totally dominated Ahab's will, authority, and power. Ahab turned into the puppet of Jezebel, who is widely recognized as the most prolific narcissist in the Bible.

The most popular record of their interaction as a couple, is found in 1 KINGS 19:1-2. It states: *And Ahab told Jezebel all that Elijah had done, and withal how he had slain all the prophets with the sword. Then Jezebel sent a messenger unto Elijah, saying, So let the gods do to me, and more also, if I make not thy life as the life of one of them by tomorrow about this time.*

Jezebel simply consumed the power of Ahab; she dominated his will and erased his identity. If Ahab were not such a weak codependent, Jezebel could not have accomplished the harm she created.

Narcissistic Spouses Will Usurp the Power and Authority of Their Partner to Hurt Others.

When we look at the cruel nature of Jezebel, one can only imagine what it must have been like to be confined to close quarters with her daily. Narcissists are so unrelenting they wear their objects down until there's a total surrender—a confrontation that makes the narcissist leave or a complete departure by the spouse from the relationship.

There Is No Attainment of Mutual Respect or Coming to an Understanding with a Narcissist.

This is simply my opinion based on my observations. One either surrenders to a zombie-like state of obedience to the narcissist or one maintains their personal dignity and identity and moves on from the dysfunction of it all. There is no place for mutual understanding or compromise.

THE CHALLENGES OF A NARCISSISTIC MARRIAGE:

1. YOU'LL CONSTANTLY HAVE TO EXPLAIN YOURSELF REGARDING COMMON-SENSE ISSUES

A narcissistic spouse will maintain a constant and intentional atmosphere of drama and misunderstanding.

You will feel like you're making mistakes and doing something wrong constantly. The more you attempt to explain yourself, the less they will seem to understand and the more confused you become. It's not that they don't get it. They are intentionally generating confusion. It's mind manipulation.

Narcissists Thrive on Other People's Confusion.

The narcissist creates confusion around you intentionally. They will constantly gaslight you to make you feel stupid or crazy. They will have you wondering if you are insane.

The Bible says in 1 PETER 5:8, *Be sober, be vigilant; because your adversary the devil, as a roaring lion, walketh about, seeking whom he may devour.*

The narcissist is driven by the spirit of Lucifer, who I believe to be the original type of narcissist. Satan devours by confusing the mind and perverting the judgment of people. The narcissist has an agenda to confuse and frustrate their spouse.

2. YOU'LL ALWAYS FEEL LIKE YOU'RE LIVING BETWEEN CALM AND STORM

When one is joined to a narcissist, the climate of the house will go from peaceful to volatile in moments. You'll never know what to expect. It can give you ulcers if you take it seriously.

There is a record in MARK 5:1–9, which says: *And they came over unto the other side of the sea, into the country of the Gadarenes. And when he was come out of the ship, immediately there met him out of the tombs a man with an unclean spirit, Who had his dwelling among the tombs; and no man could bind him, no, not with chains: Because that he had been often bound with fetters and chains, and the chains had been plucked asunder by him, and the fetters broken in pieces: neither could any man tame him. And always, night and day, he was in the mountains, and in the tombs, crying, and cutting himself with stones. But when he saw Jesus afar off, he ran and worshipped him, And cried with a loud voice, and said, What have I to do with thee, Jesus, thou Son of the most high God? I adjure thee by God, that thou torment me not. For he said unto him, Come out of the man, thou unclean spirit. And he asked him, What is thy name? And he answered, saying, My name is Legion: for we are many.*

The comparison I want to draw at this point is how the man in the tombs went from violent and dangerous to docile. He was being managed by a legion of spirits. The experience of living with a narcissist can be quite similar to these people's horrific encounter with this demoniac. The climate is never stable and settled; it's always swinging between extremes.

3. YOU WILL NEVER FIND AFFIRMATION WITHIN YOUR MARRIAGE BECAUSE THEY WILL NEVER CELEBRATE YOU

The narcissist requires self-esteem and finds a false sense of it by draining everyone else's self-esteem through calculated and intentional behavior. One way they do this is by refusing to congratulate or celebrate your accomplishments. They cannot celebrate your achievements because they feel as though your advancement only serves to diminish them. In other words, they can't celebrate you because they hate themselves.

Affirmation and support are needs you'll rarely have met in a marriage with a narcissist. It is not in them (the narcissist) to give you affirmation or to esteem you. This becomes the single greatest need in spouses of narcissists—they are never nurtured with affirmations and celebration.

The Lack of Affirmation Also Accounts for the Many Outside Affairs of Spouses of Narcissists.

I have seen extramarital affairs develop more than a few times because one party could not nurture their spouse sufficiently. On a few occasions, I am comfortable in saying these people were married to individuals who were self-consumed and failed to provide the intangible elements of affection, affirmation, and attention to their marriages.

There's a record of religious narcissists giving the Apostle Paul a hard time. It's found in ACTS 13:44–45, and it says: *And the next sabbath day came almost the whole city together to hear the word of God. But when the Jews saw the multitudes, they were filled with envy, and spake against those things which were spoken by Paul, contradicting and blaspheming.*

The Jews were a band of narcissists. The Bible says that when they saw Paul's success in getting the people's attention, they were filled with envy. This is fundamental to a narcissistic response in relationships. A narcissist gets very envious of their spouse's success. The text went on to say that they spoke against the work of Paul. Narcissistic spouses will absolutely poison your environment with negative words. They will also contradict your character before your circle. It will be like sleeping with the enemy.

4. THEY MAY ACCUSE YOU OF RIDICU- LOUS AND CRAZY THINGS TO MISREPRESENT YOU TO YOUR FAMILY AND FRIENDS

I have made no secret about the fact that I view the narcissistic spirit as the spawn of Lucifer. Accusations are Lucifer's mode of operation. The Bible says in REVELATION 12:10, *And I heard a loud voice saying in heaven, Now, is come salvation, and strength, and the kingdom of our God, and the power of his Christ: for the accuser of our brethren is cast down, which accused them before our God day and night.*

Lucifer is the accuser of the brothers, and so are narcissists. They can create a storyline around your life that will make your own family look at you sideways. They are masterful liars because they practice a lot. Narcissists have been responsible for destroying great careers with detailed lies that demolished good people with stellar reputations.

5. THEY PRACTICE PASSIVE-AGGRESSIVE DOMINATION

The narcissistic spouse is the master of making their partner feel bad. There will be some smart remarks made after every opinion you share. Every idea you have will be made to seem stupid. Whatever you might do and feel good about will be shot down immediately.

The Narcissist Dominates the Moment Whenever Others Are Feeling Great About Anything.

The word of God states something about David and his wife that is very telling. It's in 2 SAMUEL 6:18–22, and it says: *And as soon as David had made an end of offering burnt offerings and peace offerings, he blessed the people in the name of the Lord of hosts. And he dealt among all the people, even among the whole multitude of Israel, as well to the women as men, to everyone a cake of bread, and a good piece of flesh, and a flagon of wine. So all the people departed everyone to his house.*

Then David returned to bless his household. And Michal the daughter of Saul came out to meet David, and said, How glorious was the king of Israel to day, who uncovered himself to day in the eyes of the handmaids of his servants, as one of the vain fellows shamelessly uncovers himself! And David said unto Michal, It was before the Lord, which chose me before thy father, and before all his house, to appoint me ruler over the people of the Lord, over Israel: therefore will I play before the Lord. And I will yet be more vile than thus, and will be base in mine own sight: and of the maidservants which thou hast spoken of, of them shall I be had in honor.

David's wife was using passive-aggressive tactics to rob him of his personal joy. She ridiculed his exuberant demonstration of praise. David countered her attack with these words: "I will be worse next time." His response was funny to me. It sounds like something I would say.

Whenever You're Dealing with a Condescending, Passive-Aggressive Narcissist, Always Take the Power Back with a Response That Is Totally Unexpected by Them. Leave Them Scratching Their Heads.

HOW TO SURVIVE A NARCISSISTIC MARRIAGE

A. YOU MUST REALIZE THAT YOUR MARRIAGE IS AN EXERCISE IN PSYCHOLOGICAL AND SPIRITUAL WARFARE

While most people have marriages where they can relate sincerely and consistently to each other, a marriage to a narcissist is like a constant game of hide-and-seek.

The word of God says in 2 CORINTHIANS 10:3, *For though we walk in the flesh, we do not war after the flesh: (For the weapons of our warfare are not carnal, but mighty through God to the pulling down of strong holds;)*

For some, spiritual concepts may feel like a stretch. You may not be very religious or even spiritual; however, when you think about the depths of deceit and maliciousness that many narcissists generate, how else might it be explained, other than being demonic? I do not believe that the innate human spirit alone can create the pain and hurt that some of these narcissists create. Just as there's a level of goodness in man that is obviously God working through them, there's a level of malignancy that transcends the person and reveals a diabolical influence.

When you realize and accept that you are possibly dealing with demonic spirits, you are in a much better space to process all of the data that will flood your head.

Narcissists Create Very Vivid and Destructive Imaginations in Their Victims. When You Understand This, You Can Begin to Cast These Imaginations Down.

B. YOU MUST RELINQUISH YOUR DREAM OF HAVING AN IDEAL MARRIAGE

You do not have an ideal marriage when you are joined to a narcissist. Your world is filled with selfishness, competition, and emotional warfare. The sooner you forget about the fantasy and get to know this person, the sooner you can figure out if you have the grace to live with all of the emotional neglect you will face.

You Must Possess a Very High Self-Esteem That Insulates Your Soul.

There's a very interesting story in the Bible about a prophet that God instructed to marry a less-than-ideal woman. The Prophet Hosea married a woman named Gomer, and I believe that she was a narcissist. She happened to be a prostitute. After Hosea gave her a life she never dreamed of, she still left him to go back into the streets to sell her body to men. You cannot make your marriage ideal when you're dealing with a narcissist. Marriage requires the participation of two equal parties making an equal contribution. A narcissist is incapable of harmonizing in a selfless endeavor. Though Hosea gave everything, she took what he gave and still did what pleased her, even though it broke his heart. She did not care.

The Bible says in HOSEA 3:1-3, *Then said the Lord unto me, Go yet, love a woman beloved of her friend, yet an adulteress, according to the love of the Lord toward the children of Israel, who look to other gods, and love flagons of wine. So I bought her to me for fifteen pieces of silver, and for an homer of barley, and an half homer of barley: And I said unto her, Thou shalt abide for me many days; thou shalt not play the harlot, and thou shalt not be for another man: so will I also be for thee.*

This marriage between Hosea and Gomer was riddled with infidelity, selfishness, sabotage, and emotional abuse. The interesting fact in this story is that Hosea knew what he was dealing with. God told him who Gomer was before he married her. Hosea had no ideal fantasy in mind. He was completely aware of what he was in for. It is very important that people who are involved in marriages with narcissists know what they are dealing with and not fantasize about an ideal. That may be self-destructive.

C. YOU MUST INSULATE YOUR MIND FROM THE POISON

I once had a conversation with a particular spouse who was torn between leaving or staying in a marriage with a narcissist. Being a Christian myself and sharing the same values regarding marriage, I understood. My advice to them was that they would have to insulate their soul if they would not isolate themselves from the narcissist. By *isolate*, I mean to leave and separate themselves from the toxic environment.

To insulate the mind means to adjust your mind in a way where you can be physically present and emotionally detached. This is hard to do because it goes against everything a marital relationship is built on. Marriage is normally about communion and transparency, but when you are tied to a narcissist, it becomes a survival mission. If you are going to stay in the situation, you must protect your mind.

We do this through meditation and self-talk. Meditation is simply the process of choosing your focus. When navigating a toxic marriage, you must check out of reality and mentally go to a place that calms and inspires you. For some, this is accomplished through reading the Bible, quiet walks, prayer time, or anything that produces peace and positivity.

The self-talk concept is exactly what it sounds like: You talk to yourself to create intentional beliefs. When a person is in proximity to a narcissist, their self-esteem and value are constantly being compromised. The individual must learn to build themselves up with their internal conversation. When there are no preachers, counselors, or motivational speakers, you must learn how to talk to yourself to rebuild areas that have been torn down.

There is a biblical record of King David being in a situation where everyone around him wanted to kill him, and the Bible says, "David encouraged himself."

It is recorded in 1 SAMUEL 30:6: *And David was greatly distressed; for the people spake of stoning him, because the soul of all the people was grieved, every man for his sons and for his daughters: but David encouraged himself in the Lord his God.*

We must all learn to encourage ourselves, especially those who are tied to narcissists.

D. YOU MUST PRACTICE BEING EMOTIONALLY UNPREDICTABLE

This simply means that you never react in a way that they are expecting or would assume. If it is a matter that should call for anger, smile and respond pleasantly. If you should be very concerned, behave like it's no big deal.

Your Authentic Emotions Cannot Be on Display to People Who Will Hurt You with Them.

Jesus Christ practiced this. When they were judging and abusing Him, the Bible says He did not say a word. You must never be predictable with people who intend to hurt you.

When you can restrain your emotions, you maintain the power. The person who can manage their emotions is the master. Though you are not attempting to manage or control the emotions of the narcissistic spouse, you definitely do not want them to exercise that control over you.

There's an interesting passage of scripture that is most applicable in this instance. It is found in PROVERBS 24:7, which says: *Wisdom is too high for a fool. When you conceal your emotional buttons, you elevate the game to a level that the narcissist cannot reach.*

E. NEVER UNDERESTIMATE HOW FAR THEY WILL GO

Never underestimate how far they may go when you are in the grips of a narcissist's marriage. In other words, don't assume they will never get violent or won't take all of the money out of the accounts. Never say never. You do not really know this person. Consequently, you do not know how far they will take it when they feel like they have lost control. Be prepared for your most horrific nightmare. Never ever underestimate how far they may go, and know when to retreat.

There's a jewel of wisdom found in PROVERBS 15:1: *A soft answer turneth away wrath: but grievous words stir up anger.*

There will be days that you will need to monitor the climate and adjust your behavior accordingly. If it comes to a worst-case scenario, how would you deal with it?

F. LET THEM GO WHEN THEY WANT TO LEAVE

When you stop dancing to the beat of the narcissist's drum, they will get frustrated and probably attempt to leave at a certain point. *Do not stop them!* Do not behave like it's time to party, but don't act like you're going to fall apart if they leave. Simply be emotionally unpredictable and let them go.

CHAPTER 7

THE MENTAL GAMES NARCISSISTS PLAY

The most confusing predicament one might find themselves in is being in a relationship with a narcissist. Even a casual encounter with a narcissist can prove to be puzzling. While the sincere and good-intentioned individual is approaching the situation from an honest and purposeful platform, the narcissist is devising and calculating schemes to confuse, manage, and manipulate. At worst, the narcissist may even go as far as intentionally driving the victim insane, if possible. At the very least, the narcissist strives to deceive and confuse.

Confusing Others Is the Entertainment of the Narcissist.

For a normal and well-adjusted individual, a relationship is an opportunity to give as much as one might take. A relationship is a context in which we may become vulnerable with others and build authentic structures of trust. It is not the same for a narcissist.

For a narcissist, a relationship is an opportunity to deceive, trick, and manipulate another individual. It is the context in which the narcissist plays a role, makes the other party in the relationship believe the act, and finally destroys that individual's life and soul (emotional stability).

Everything with the narcissist is about gaining an advantage over others through tactics of control and manipulation. They are like mind-control experts, and everything is a game.

The unsuspecting victim will think that they are simply engaged in a normal conversation, only to discover later they were being psychologically managed the entire time.

The Bible records an incident that depicts how this process often goes. It was the occasion when the snake in the Garden of Eden tricked Eve and Adam.

In GENESIS 3:1–5, it states: *Now the serpent was more subtil than any beast of the field which the Lord God had made. And he said unto the woman, Yea, hath God said, Ye shall not eat of every tree of the garden? And the woman said unto the serpent, We may eat of the fruit of the trees of the garden: But of the fruit of the tree which is in the midst of the garden, God hath said, Ye shall not eat of it, neither shall ye touch it, lest ye die. And the serpent said unto the woman, Ye shall not surely die: For God doth know that in the day ye eat thereof, then your eyes shall be opened, and ye shall be as gods, knowing good and evil.*

If you read the full context of this text, you'll see how the serpent took the instructions that God gave to Adam and Eve, and he twisted them to such a degree that both Adam and Eve became confused. When Satan completed his mission, he talked Adam and Eve out of their place of dominion. He also destroyed their fellowship with God. Satan robbed them of their abundance, and he wrecked their connection to God. I believe that this represents two outcomes when encountering and entertaining a narcissist.

When Narcissists Are Done, They May Leave the Victim Depleted Emotionally, and Their Vital Relationships May Be in Shambles.

Notice how Satan produced all of this wreckage through a calculated conversation.

Talking with a narcissist is like trying to grasp a balloon in the rain that has been dipped in oil. It will wear you out, and you will never seem to make a solid connection. A conversation with a narcissist can feel like a migraine headache. The victim will struggle to get the narcissist to understand something very basic, and the narcissist will constantly allude and escape logic. They can take an easy black or white subject and turn it pink. They are always playing mental chess with others.

According to psychologists, because of some early trauma, this person's soul is deficient of empathy. They cannot feel your position nor seek to ever understand you. Something from that previous trauma made them totally consumed with themselves. Though they may have grown physically, educationally, and professionally, they are still arrested in their emotional development, which is reflected in their lack of interpersonal skills.

The word of God addresses spiritually stunted people who manifested what the equivalent of a spiritually arrested development was. It is found in HEBREWS 5:12, where it says: *For when for the time ye ought to be teachers, ye have need that one teach you again which be the first principles of the oracles of God; and are become such as have need of milk, and not of strong meat.*

When these people should have been instructors, they were still at a level where they needed basic teaching. This loosely typifies the arrested emotional development of the narcissist. The narcissist may be an adult in body and years but is still a child in their mind. Their childlike nature is demonstrated in the fact that they view life and relationships as a game where they either win or lose, and the misery of others is their greatest joy.

SOME OF THE TACTICS OF NARCISSISTS

A. THEY WILL DECLARE THEIR LOVE FOR YOU AND NEVER FOLLOW UP WITH ACTION

This is calculated. They don't really love you; they love how you make them look or feel. They love the status you bring to them. They love the financial resources you provide. They love the sexual satisfaction they get from the arrangement.

Though their love is based on an alternative motive, they can make you feel like they really love you. The narcissist will profess their love for you so energetically that they will cause you to turn your back on your parents and friends.

Narcissists Are Often Excellent with Words but Pitiful on Follow-Through.

When you observe the historical records of some of the most famous narcissists, they could convince Lucifer to be baptized in the name of Jesus, but their words were empty and hollow. The real love test is in the follow-through. Narcissists sell the victim on the pitch and avoid the discussion about the delivery of the promises made.

The Bible says in 1 JOHN 3:16–18, *Hereby perceive we the love of God, because he laid down his life for us: and we ought to lay down our lives for the brethren. But whosoever hath this world's good, and seeth his brother have need, and shutteth up his bowels of compassion from him, how dwelleth the love of God in him? My little children, let us not love in word, neither in tongue; but indeed and in truth.*

A narcissist is rarely guilty of action over talk. Most narcissists will be all talk and no action. If the rare occasion happens that they actually follow through on something, it's because they need something that requires them to behave a certain way. Following through will not be a constant action in their relational profile.

B. THEY TREAT YOU LIKE THEY HATE YOU

One of the most puzzling experiences is when the narcissist goes from declarations of love to actually treating you like they hate you. After you have invested your heart and soul into the relationship, the narcissist may suddenly treat you as though you are nothing. They may treat you so poorly that you could actually begin to believe that you must deserve such treatment. It will seem to come out of nowhere.

The root of the issue is not their hatred for you—it's really a personal issue within themselves. Their apparent hatred for others is the impact of something very complicated happening in their soul.

**They Don't Really Hate You;
They Hate Themselves.**

Narcissist has a self-disdain that causes them to function antagonistically toward those persons in proximity. They hate themselves and will use others as their emotional punching bags.

The Bible includes a very interesting text. It states in TITUS 1:15: *Unto the pure all things are pure: but unto them that are defiled and unbelieving is nothing pure; but even their mind and conscience is defiled.*

A person's external perception and analysis of matters cannot transcend the level of their internal settings. A person cannot give what they don't possess, and they cannot manage the external world and their relationships beyond their self-view. For instance, if I hate myself, it's impossible for me to truly accept the idea that you love me.

When a Person's Heart Has Been Darkened So Severely, Their Entire Worldview Becomes Tainted.

The individual does not realize that the darkness they see is really emanating from within their souls. The narcissist rarely, if ever, realizes that the hatred they feel for the world is really the hatred they've inherited for themselves. Again, I say *inherited* because scientists believe narcissists are created primarily by poor or no parenting. Their conscience is defiled through irreparable conditioning. You must never take the aggressive and resentful behavior of narcissists personally; it is their issue, not yours.

C. THEY WILL HUMILIATE YOU

Another common experience one might have in a marriage with a narcissist is the feeling of humiliation. They will do everything possible to break your confidence and diminish you in people's eyes. They will humiliate you before your family, friends, and even coworkers.

The worst experience is when they humiliate you and behave as if they don't know what they've done. I guess we could call this passive humiliation.

One example I can remember is when I had a married couple with very private marital issues. Nobody knew what was happening, and the details were contained within the couple and me as their pastor. One evening I started getting calls was some very private information being distributed across social media relating to this couple. One of the individuals took it upon themselves to broadcast and humiliate the other party with totally private information.

When I saw this childish display of vindictiveness, I immediately recognized the narcissistic undertone. This did not express a desire to rectify the issue or to restore the marriage. This was not merely about being hurt. This was about breaking the soul of their partner. This was about coming out looking like the victim and assuring that their spouse would be criticized by society. This was about emotional abuse. Of course, I was not too pleased with these actions and demanded they remove all information posted on social media. My wishes were reluctantly followed.

Narcissists Humiliate Others Because They Need to Diminish the Other Person to Elevate Themselves.

Humiliation is one of the chief tactics of Satan. The Bible usually refers to his antics as accusations. Satan spends a lot of time accusing others to generate guilt in the accused. After guilt has been established, he proceeds to manage and control the person.

One portion of scripture says in REVELATION 12:10, *And I heard a loud voice saying in heaven, now is come salvation, and strength, and the kingdom of our God, and the power of his Christ: for the accuser of our brethren is cast down, which accused them before our God day and night.*

We see from this text that Satan practices accusing others, night and day. He is so committed to accusing others he does it even before God, who knows better.

Like Satan, the narcissist is relentless in humiliating his victim. For the victim, this may feel like waves of negativity and emotional abuse that never seem to cease.

The narcissist is committed to breaking the soul of his victim.

D. THEY APOLOGIZE PROFUSELY, BUT NOTHING EVER CHANGES

Nobody can destroy you like a narcissist, and nobody can pull you back in like a narcissist. The narcissist can shoot you seven times, at point blank range, while you're positioned beneath a spotlight, and convince you that it was a mistake, they did not know it was you, and they are deeply sorrowful. You'll find yourself leaving the hospital and going home with the same narcissist that tried to kill you.

It almost seems like the narcissist is a hypnotist. They can lie and apologize their way out of anything. It feels like their words are like tentacles reaching into your conscious mind and managing your thoughts. You may declare that you are done, finished, and you're not going to be talked out of it, but once they corner you, your mind is changed.

The Problem with the Apology of the Narcissist Is That *It Is a Lie!*

They are not sorry, and they will not change. Many victims of narcissistic abuse go a lifetime and never learn the difference between an empty apology and actually being sorry.

The Bible clearly distinguishes between sincere sorrow and an apology designed to manage a moment and to manipulate a victim. In 2 CORINTHIANS 7:10 it says: *For godly sorrow worketh repentance to salvation not to be repented of: but the sorrow of the world worketh death.*

When the text talks about godly sorrow working repentance, it communicates that a person who is truly sorry changes their behavior. Repentance always accompanies any sincere apology. A person who is truly sorry changes what they do. The narcissist makes great declarations of sorrow but never changes. People often hear the same old worn-out apology for decades before they wake up.

E. WHEN YOU BEGIN TO PULL AWAY, THEY MAKE YOU FEEL GUILTY AND ACCUSE YOU OF ABANDONING THEM

A person may realize that the relationship is futile and even lose their attraction to the narcissist. When they pull away to break free, another web the narcissist will spin to trap the victim is the web of guilt. The narcissist may go as far as to launch a social media campaign painting themselves as having been abandoned by someone they trusted. They will send confusing text messages like: "How could you do this to me?" The reality may be that they physically assaulted you, but somehow you are doing this to them. They will often resort to threats of suicide. All of this is to guilt the victim into submission. *Do not fall for it!*

It's probably best to avoid having any conversation with a narcissist after you've made up your mind that you're done. Just be finished with it, and don't be moved by the victimization propaganda.

SOME OF THE CLASSIC NARCISSISTIC ABUSE TACTICS

The following descriptions are among the classic behaviors of narcissists in relationships. These are the things that counselors and therapists are searching to identify within your relationship as they ask you a series of questions. I encourage you to study these concepts further. This book is written to awaken your consciousness to a subliminal warfare that you may not have even detected you were in.

Beyond this, you should seek to educate yourself at the feet of those who are authorities in these matters.

1. LOVE BOMBING

A basic human need is self-esteem. Most people have not been properly trained in how to actually esteem themselves. This fact leaves most people vulnerable to emotional vampires, who latch on to the esteem deficiency and pretend to fill the void. The problem is that they are not filling a void—they are creating an addiction.

Love Bombing Is the Intentional Process of Creating an Emotional Addiction in a Victim.

Basically, love bombing consists of giving someone a lot of positive attention and affection. It is not sincere, but it feels real. In my book, *The Father Daughter Talk*, I write about how the womanizing man overdoses the woman on everything she's ever dreamed of in a romantic relationship. He does this to become the woman's emotional addiction. Once she's addicted, the toxic bond is established; she's trapped.

The Purpose of Love Bombing Is to Turn Your Emotions Up High to Dull Your Intelligence and Spiritual Discernment.

Love bombing makes the situation feel like the perfect relationship. The victim makes declarations like: "I've never been so happy" or "You are the partner of my dreams." The intent of the love bombing is to create a deceptive cloud of euphoria. The victim can't think, pray, or hear reasoning.

The Bible states in PROVERBS 16:25, *There is a way that seemeth right unto a man, but the end thereof are the ways of death.*

Some of the most disastrous relationships in history started out like a literal dream.

Love Bombing Feels Good Until It Doesn't.

There's a passage of biblical text that I reference quite frequently in my writings. You're going to witness in these verses is a classic case of love bombing and the tragic end. This is absolutely worth the read. What

In PROVERBS 7:6–23 it says: *For at the window of my house I looked through my casement, And beheld among the simple ones, I discerned among the youths, a young man void of understanding, Passing through the street near her corner; and he went the way to her house, In the twilight, in the evening, in the black and dark night: And, behold, there met him a woman with the attire of a harlot, and subtle of heart. (She is loud and stubborn; her feet abide not in her house: Now is she without, now in the streets, and lieth in wait at every corner.) So she caught him, and kissed him, and with an impudent face said unto him, I have peace offerings with me; this day have I paid my vows. Therefore came I forth to meet thee, diligently to seek thy face, and I have found thee. I have decked my bed with coverings of tapestry, with carved works, with fine linen of Egypt. I have perfumed my bed with myrrh, aloes, and cinnamon. Come, let us take our fill of love until the morning: let us solace ourselves with loves. For the goodman is not at home, he is gone a long journey: He hath taken a bag of money with him and will come home at the day appointed. With her much fair speech she caused him to yield, with the flattering of her lips she forced him. He goeth after her straightway, as an ox goeth to the slaughter, or as a fool to the correction of the stocks; Till a dart strike through his liver; as a bird hasteth to the snare, and knoweth not that it is for his life.*

Wow! In this text, we see a young, simple man, void of understanding, being love bombed by an experienced harlot. She seduces him with flattery and descriptions of a sexual encounter until he divorces himself from all judgment or discretion. The text concludes with the fact that this lapse in discretion may cost the young man his very life. He was love bombed.

When the Smoke from the Love Bomb Clears, the Reality of Bondage and Entrapment Appears.

Suddenly, what felt like adoration and ecstasy begins to feel like stalking or a prison sentence. The person who was your dream has now become your nightmare. When the smoke of the love bomb fades, you begin to see the true colors of the diabolic actor that lured you into his trap.

The Narcissist Can Act Good Enough, Long Enough, to Get You Emotionally Addicted. After the Addiction Comes the Withdrawal.

In PROVERBS 6:25–26 it states: *Lust not after her beauty in thine heart; neither let her take thee with her eyelids. For by means of a whorish woman a man is brought to a piece of bread: and the adulteress will hunt for the precious life.*

The person you thought you knew, and the life you thought you were building together, have been shattered into a million little fragments. You've gone from fantasy to reality.

The love bombing gave you a false sense of fulfillment, esteem, and security. You could finally exhale. When reality struck, your sense of self was eroded and diminished. You were idolized, then shoved off the pedestal.

2. HOOVERING

The term hoovering is named after the Hoover vacuum cleaner. It speaks of how the narcissistic abuser finds a way to keep sucking the victim back into the trap.

Whenever There Is a Breakup with a Narcissist, They Are Plotting How They May Re-enter the Victim's Life Again When It Is Beneficial to Them. They Go Away— But They Never Go Away.

The narcissist may go away for a while to explore another victim or to plunder new territory, but they always have a plan to resurface when it's convenient for them. When they resurface, they use tactics like reminiscing over the good times or using the children. They may even use spirituality if that is valuable in the victim's life. They will talk about how they accepted God and God wants them to make it right. While hoovering, they will then do everything they should have been doing.

Hoovering also correlates with a demonic tendency described in the Bible.

It is found in MATTHEW 12:43–45: *When the unclean spirit is gone out of a man, he walketh through dry places, seeking rest, and finlet none. Then he saith, I will return into my house from whence I came out; and when he is come, he findeth it empty, swept, and garnished. Then goeth he, and taketh with himself seven other spirits more wicked than himself, and they enter in and dwell there: and the last state of that man is worse than the first.*

Notice how the demonic spirit will leave, circle back to see if there is still an opening, and come back with even greater intensity. The Bible says that the last state of that man is worse than before.

This is the demonic tendency of the narcissist. They will propose to leave, circle back, and return with an even greater vengeance.

If the victim allows the narcissist back in, the narcissist will simply strengthen the toxic bond between the two of them and leave again when it is convenient to do so.

**Every Time a Narcissist Is Successful
with Hoovering, the Victim Is Being More
Severely Damaged and Is Less Likely to Move
on to Another, Healthier Relationship.**

The only defense one has against the hoovering tactic is to absolutely make no time or space for the narcissist. You don't need to talk through direct messages or texting.

You don't need to engage in small talk, and if there are children, the conversation needs to be about the business of parenting.

The Bible says in EPHESIANS 4:27, *Neither give place to the devil.*

The hoovering only works when there is space given for the narcissist to operate. If you make no time or space for the narcissist, the hoovering cannot succeed.

Narcissists hoover for many reasons. I believe that they hoover and don't simply move on, like normal people, because they need to feel as though they are significant to someone. Whenever they come back into your life, and you don't resist them, it fuels their twisted sense of self-worship.

3. GHOSTING

There is another tactic that is in the narcissist's arsenal that is extremely effective at destroying the self-esteem and will of their victim. It's called ghosting.

Ghosting Is When the Narcissist Suddenly Disappears from the Life of the Person They Are in a Relationship with for No Apparent Reason.

For example, the narcissist will pursue a person sexually for months; they will love bomb them; and, finally, when they've accomplished their Mephistophelian (devilish) agenda, they'll become hard to reach. In some cases, they will immediately drop off the face of the earth. They won't return calls. They won't come around. Then at some random time, they will begin hoovering.

The Purpose of Ghosting Is to Break the Confidence and Independence of the Victim.

Ghosting is mental combat. It's a war to control the relationship through demeaning, disregarding, and disrespecting. Just when the victim thinks they have a legitimate relationship, the other part of this "relationship" has not called and won't return a call. What can that do to self-esteem?

Ghosting is not only a tactic used in romantic relation-ships, but it is also a narcissistic practice in friendships and even relationships in groups, like a church. As a pastor, I have seen people disappear from the church without a trace. Nobody knew what happened, or if we had done something wrong.

When a person can just disappear without a conver-sation or confrontation, it is a power move intended to manipulate your emotions or injure your self-esteem.

The Bible provides a powerful biblical principle that serves as a psychological response to people walking out of your life without cause.

In 1 JOHN 2:19, it states: *They went out from us, but they were not of us; for if they had been of us, they would no doubt have continued with us: but they went out, that they might be made manifest that they were not all of us.*

The Only Mental Recourse One Has Against Ghosting Is Acceptance and Progression.

We must accept people's right to move on, and we, too, must move on past them. They will still be present if they were meant to be a part of your future. It may hurt, but it is absolutely necessary to accept reality. The last thing you want to do is to be in a posture where you are trying to figure out what they are thinking or what you could have done wrong. Let it go.

4. GASLIGHTING

Gaslighting is a tactic in which a person or entity, in order to gain power, makes a victim question their reality and sanity. The narcissist does things intentionally gauged to drive the victim insane.

The Purpose of Gaslighting Is to Create an Enormous Inner Storm of Confusion Between What's True and False.

The term *gaslighting* originates from the 1944 movie entitled *Gaslight*. In the movie, a man manipulates situations to the point where his wife thinks she is losing her mind.

Gaslighting involves the manipulation of facts and reality to make the victim believe a false truth. The closest biblical example I could think of is Jezebel's manipulation of Elijah's mind after his great victory over her army of false prophets. He had already won, but somehow Jezebel convinced him that she could kill him. She gaslighted him.

The incident is recorded in 1 KINGS 19:2-4, where it says, *Then Jezebel sent a messenger unto Elijah, saying, So let the gods do to me, and more also, if I make not thy life as the life of one of them by tomorrow about this time. And when he saw that, he arose, and went for his life, and came to Beersheba, which belongeth to Judah, and left his servant there. But he himself went a day's journey into the wilderness, and came and sat down under a juniper tree: and he requested for himself that he might die; and said, It is enough; now, O Lord, take away my life; for I am not better than my fathers.*

Notice how Jezebel's words made Elijah divorce himself from a clear reality and buy into a false version.

5. TRIANGULATION

Triangulation is when the narcissist positions between two parties to control the narrative. The narcissist will feed calculated information to each party with the explicit intention of being the puppet master of both. The narcissist will create doubts in each about the other and paint themselves as the go-to person for both. The narcissist strives to become the most trusted within the triangle.

Triangulation happens in workplace settings between coworkers. It happens in families and anywhere people are. The narcissist finds a way to puppet people without anyone knowing the difference. The people are the actors, while the narcissist is the secret playwright.

Triangulation is often the energy behind many arguments and confusion in certain circles. People sometimes never get to the bottom of why their relationships deterio-rate. The narcissist was behind the entire operation.

6. FLYING MONKEYS

The last tactic we will look at is called flying monkeys. This term is borrowed from the 1939 classic film, *The Wizard of Oz*. The Wicked Witch of the West sent flying monkeys to terrorize the citizens in the film. The concept of flying monkeys speaks of people who are the puppets of malignant narcissists, who go in and out of the lives of third parties to exact the narcissist's abuse. Some refer to this as abuse by proxy.

We see many flying monkeys in the life of the biblical character Jezebel. Her husband, King Ahab, was the main tool she used to inflict punishment on others. We also see the army of prophets to Baal, who were her flying monkeys. These were an organized group of religious leaders to promote Jezebel's agenda. This was the group that Elijah defeated by the power of God. This is why their deaths angered Jezebel so much.

A biblical story captures the essence of a flying monkey beautifully; it's the interesting story of King Herod, John the Baptist, and Herod's wife, Herodias. Herodias was Herod's brother's former wife, which made their union immoral. The Prophet John made a public outcry concerning their arrangement. Herodias wanted to kill John, but Herod feared the political backlash; John was loved by a lot of people. Herod elected to imprison John instead. Herodias wanted him dead and used a flying monkey to accomplish her agenda. Read the following account and see if you can detect the flying monkey.

It is recorded in MARK 6:17–28: *For Herod himself had sent forth and laid hold upon John, and bound him in prison for Herodias' sake, his brother Philip's wife: for he had married her. For John had said unto Herod, It is not lawful for thee to have thy brother's wife. Therefore, Herodias had a quarrel against him, and would have killed him; but she could not: For Herod feared John, knowing that he was a just man and an holy, and observed him; and when he heard him, he did many things, and heard him gladly. And when a convenient day was come, that Herod on his birthday made a supper to his lords, high captains, and chief estates of Galilee; And when the daughter of the said Herodias came in, and danced, and pleased Herod and them that sat with him, the king said unto the damsel, Ask of me whatsoever thou wilt, and I will give it thee. And he sware unto her, Whatsoever thou shalt ask of me, I will give it thee, unto the half of my kingdom. And she went forth, and said unto her mother, What shall I ask? And she said, The head of John the Baptist. And she came in straightway with haste unto the king, and asked, saying, I will that thou give me by and by in a charger the head of John the Baptist. And the king was exceeding sorry; yet for his oath's sake, and for their sakes which sat with him, he would not reject her. And immediately the king sent an executioner, and commanded his head to be brought: and he went and beheaded him in the prison, And brought his head in a charger, and gave it to the damsel: and the damsel gave it to her mother.*

Do you see the monkey? When Herodias could not accomplish her fiendish agenda on her own, she used her daughter, Salome, as a flying monkey to manipulate her husband into doing what she wanted him to do.

CHAPTER 8

AN
EXIT
STRATEGY
FROM
A
NARCISSIST

Toxic people have a talent for entangling others into a web of codependency. The victim can't get free even when they want to. It becomes a bond that functions like a glue trap for insects. They walk into it, but it won't allow them to walk out. They get stuck in place; it's ultimately designed to kill them. The narcissist goes to great extremes to keep their victims tied up.

The Narcissist Works to Maintain This Toxic Bond Because of an Inexplicable Level of Anger.

Narcissists are driven and motivated by anger. They are angry with their parents in certain instances. They are angry with the people who possess the lives they covet. They are angry with the people who escaped their grips. They are angry with themselves, and they are angry with their most immediate victims.

If you happen to be the focus of the narcissist's immediate attention, they are wrapping their very angry paws around your life. At an appointed time, their anger will always manifest.

The reason they hurt you over and over again and tell you how worthless you are and still won't release you is that they have an angry agenda concerning you. They want to destroy everything good in your life, and the only way to accomplish this is to hold on to you until they can finish the job.

The Bible puts it plainly in PROVERBS 22:24–25: *Make no friendship with an angry man; and with a furious man thou shalt not go: Lest thou learn his ways and get a snare to thy soul.*

The Bible says that we should not consider having a relationship with an angry person. The passage culminates by expressing that a connection to the angry individual can lead to a snare of your soul. Soul refers to your mind, will, and emotion caught in a trap of enmeshment (a situation nearly impossible to escape).

HOW DOES ONE BREAK FREE FROM THE TRAP?

It Takes Wisdom to Know How to Walk Out of the Snare of a Narcissist.

A narcissist is not operating with normal thought patterns. This is not normal psychology you're dealing with. There's a satanic influence that accompanies every move the narcissist makes. They are always three steps ahead of you. The only solution is to tap into the wisdom of God when dealing with the narcissist.

The Bible teaches a powerful principle in PROVERBS 24:7, which says: *Wisdom is too high for a fool: he openeth not his mouth in the gate.*

When detangling yourself from a narcissistic trap, you must activate the spirit of wisdom.

When a Victim Begins to Suddenly Respond in Wisdom as Opposed to Reacting in Frustration, the Narcissist Is Left Confused.

When you elevate your responses to a level of wisdom with the narcissist, it is similar to how a charging dog reacts to a person who stands still and stares down; the dog will usually stop in its tracks and go away. The dog is accustomed to creating a reaction. When it gets a confident authoritarian-like response, it has to rethink and regroup because it's not sure about who it is dealing with.

The Spirit of Wisdom Is Too Advanced for a Narcissist.

The obvious question at this point has to be, where does wisdom come from? The Bible has something very specific to say about how wisdom is attained.

In JAMES 1:5 it says: *If any of you lack wisdom, let him ask of God, that giveth to all men liberally, and upbraideth not; and it shall be given him.*

The Bible says that a person should pray and ask God for wisdom when needed. The reality of a person who lives within narcissistic abuse is that they are so stressed and terrified they never think to actually pray and ask God for help.

The devastating reality of the predicament is that the person is engaged in diabolical and spiritual warfare and is trying to survive with natural weapons. The Bible says in 2 CORINTHIANS 10:3, *For though we walk in the flesh, we do not war after the flesh. For the weapons of our warfare are not carnal, but mighty through God to the pulling down of strong holds.*

The engagement with the narcissist must be understood as deeply spiritual and demonic. When you understand this truth, you'll be prepared to get out of the realm of your carnal mind and engage this individual spiritually, by the power of God.

When You Recognize God as Your Only Source, Wisdom Begins.

When you are escaping a narcissist, you will definitely need divine wisdom.

There's the story of David avoiding King Saul's malignant narcissistic rage. Saul had gotten jealous of David and felt like David was showing him up. This drove Saul into a furious, murderous state of anger against David. David did nothing but serve Saul and honor him.

The incident is found in 1 SAMUEL 18:12–16. It says: *And Saul was afraid of David, because the Lord was with him, and was departed from Saul. Therefore Saul removed him from him, and made him his captain over a thousand; and he went out and came in before the people. And David behaved himself wisely in all his ways; and the Lord was with him. Wherefore when Saul saw that he behaved himself very wisely, he was afraid of him. But all Israel and Judah loved David, because he went out and came in before them.*

Notice how David behaved himself very wisely with Saul. It will take wisdom to escape the trap of narcissistic control. This text also reveals a major reason we must exercise uncommon wisdom: The Bible says that Saul was afraid of David. Saul was king and had all of the power, yet he was afraid of David.

**Most Narcissists Are Driven by an Underlying
Fear, Which Makes Them Very Dangerous.
This Fear Generates a Paranoia That
Demands Wisdom to Circumvent.**

THE STRATEGY

1. BREAK THE GRIP OF FEAR

Narcissists are generally scared, little cowards. They will if they can create a false perception of dominance over you. They practice many tactics to impose fear on their victims. For instance, if you're married to them, they will threaten to take the kids. If you are in the public eye, they will threaten to ruin your reputation. Whatever makes you afraid is what they will do.

**You Must Courageously Reject the Fear,
In Your Conscious Mind, To Begin to
Break Their Grip on Your Life**

The Bible makes this so plain that a blind man could not miss it. In 2 TIMOTHY 1:7 it says: *For God hath not given us the spirit of fear; but of power, and of love, and of a sound mind.*

The fear you live with was not given to you by God. In other words, you were not created with a propensity to fear. The fear you're experiencing was especially delivered, compliments of the narcissist. Fear is their specialty.

COMMON AREAS WHERE THE NARCISSIST CREATES FEAR IN THEIR VICTIMS

A. FEAR OF LOST LOVE

The narcissist will plant the lie into your head that they are your last shot at love. They tell you: "No one is going to love you but me." This is to intentionally program you into submission and to subjugate your common sense.

B. FEAR OF SOCIAL RIDICULE

The narcissist paints a picture that they will smear your reputation in the circles you travel in. They paint a picture of more power than they actually possess in most cases.

Fear aids the toxic bond and creates a false sense of fear of public shame.

There's a spiritual promise found in ISAIAH 54:17; it states: *No weapon that is formed against thee shall prosper; and every tongue that shall rise against thee in judgment thou shalt condemn. This is the heritage of the servants of the Lord, and their righteousness is of me, saith the Lord.*

To break this fear will demand coming to terms with your past and not being ashamed. It will involve ignoring the comments of people who do not matter and condemning every voice that slanders you. A narcissist will need resistance at a certain point. You can't cower and play passive forever.

C. FEAR OF VIOLENCE

You will likely have to deal with the real fear of violence against you. Narcissists are some of the most volatile creatures and are subject to going from zero to a hundred in moments.

The word of God says in HEBREWS 13:6, *So that we may boldly say, The Lord is my helper, and I will not fear what man shall do unto me.*

You Must Transcend the Fear to Be Free.

King David had to deal with a great fear of King Saul. In 1 SAMUEL 18:5-11 it is recorded, and it says: *And David went out whithersoever Saul sent him, and behaved himself wisely: and Saul set him over the men of war, and he was accepted in the sight of all the people, and also in the sight of Saul's servants. And it came to pass as they came, when David was returned from the slaughter of the Philistine, that the women came out of all cities of Israel, singing and dancing, to meet king Saul, with tabrets, with joy, and with instruments of musick. And the women answered one another as they played, and said, Saul hath slain his thousands, and David his ten thousands. And Saul was very wroth, and the saying displeased him; and he said, They have ascribed unto David ten thousands, and to me they have ascribed but thousands: and what can he have more but the kingdom? And Saul eyed David from that day and forward. And it came to pass on the morrow, that the evil spirit from God came upon Saul, and he prophesied in the midst of the house: and David played with his hand, as at other times: and there was a javelin in Saul's hand. And Saul cast the javelin; for he said, I will smite David even to the wall with it. And David avoided out of his presence twice.*

The fear of physical violence is warranted when dealing with such an insecure and volatile individual. Usually, the answer to this is distance and absence.

2. BECOME EMOTIONALLY UNPREDICTABLE

The biggest advantage a narcissistic abuser has over his victim is their unbridled emotion. When your emotions are living on your sleeve, you become a puppet. I can imagine that it is extremely difficult to control the emotion that is generated by such excruciating pain. On the flip side is the reality that your emotions are the links in the chain of your captivity.

You Must Break Free Internally Before You May Go Free Physically.

The narcissist runs their life based on predicting your reactions to their antics. Always do the opposite. You must pass the internal fortitude test before you may graduate to freedom.

The Bible says in PROVERBS 25:28, *He that hath no rule over his own spirit is like a city that is broken down, and without walls.*

You are defenseless until you get a handle on your emotions.

SOME PRACTICAL SUGGESTIONS

A. BEGIN TO TALK LESS, LISTEN MORE, AND ASK MORE QUESTIONS

Your emotions are located through your conversation. When you talk less, you become unpredictable.

The word says in JAMES 1:19, *Wherefore, my beloved brethren, let every man be swift to hear, slow to speak, slow to wrath.*

B. BE PREPARED TO MAKE UNREASONABLE COMPROMISES

In the process of being emotionally indetectable, you will have to bite your tongue at times and do the exact opposite of what you feel. You cannot allow this person ever to know where you really stand. It's the ultimate poker face.

Jesus is recorded in MATTHEW 5:25 saying, *Agree with thine adversary quickly, whiles thou art in the way with him; lest at any time the adversary deliver thee to the judge, and the judge deliver thee to the officer, and thou be cast into prison.*

Notice that Jesus says to agree with them quickly before it escalates. With the narcissist, there are times it's best just to tell them that they are right and be done with the debate. They will expect you to argue and get upset but never give them the satisfaction. The aim is to make them wonder who they are dealing with.

C. DO NOT EXPOSE THEM; LET THEM SAVE THEIR PUBLIC FACE

When you have verifiable and damaging information on the narcissist, don't play your hand. They are expecting you to blast them on social media or within the mutual social circle. Don't say a word. This move will not only confuse them, but it will scare them. They will wonder what plans you have and when you will drop the hammer? They are certain that you are plotting to get even.

The Goal Is Never to Get Even—It Is to Get Out!

There's a powerful text in PROVERBS 29:11 (ESV), which states: *A fool gives full vent to his spirit, but a wise man quietly holds it back.*

NEVER PLAY YOUR HAND

3. YOU MUST BE SERIOUS ABOUT NO CONTACT

After confronting your fears, isolation is imperative for the liberation of your soul. At the time of writing this very chapter, the world is experiencing the COVID-19 pandemic. This virus is killing people daily, and it is extremely contagious. The only way to survive is to refrain from contacting other people. As we exercise social distancing, the virus is slowly dying.

There's This Rule Called the No-Contact Rule.

The rule means exactly what it says. You must cut off all communication with your ex or any narcissist. It is like getting rid of an addiction to a drug by going "cold turkey." Therefore, no contact means no text messaging, no calls, no going over, and no emails or doing anything else that boils down to getting in touch with them or allowing them to contact you.

The Most Prolific Biblical Narcissist Is Jezebel. The Prophet Elijah, Her Nemesis, Teaches Us How to Respond to Narcissistic Abuse. *Run!*

Many people want to stay and reason with the narcissist. Others want to stay and fight the narcissist. In most cases, both are bad ideas. Elijah demonstrates this. It is found in 1 KINGS 19:2–3: *Then Jezebel sent a messenger unto Elijah, saying, So let the gods do to me, and more also, if I make not thy life as the life of one of them by tomorrow about this time. And when he saw that, he arose, and went for his life, and came to Beersheba, which belongeth to Judah, and left his servant there.*

Elijah responded to Jezebel's malignant rage by leaving. He ran. He put distance between the two of them. You cannot reason with crazy, and you can't defeat the demonic.

The Bible encourages no contact in many passages. In MATTHEW 5:29–30 it says: *And if thy right eye offend thee, pluck it out, and cast it from thee: for it is profitable for thee that one of thy members should perish, and not that thy whole body should be cast into hell. And if thy right hand offend thee, cut it off, and cast it from thee: for it is profitable for thee that one of thy members should perish, and not that thy whole body should be cast into hell.*

Sometimes the preservation of your own sanity is linked to breaking contact with toxic people. In other occasions, the health of your minor children hinges on you having enough courage to eliminate certain people from your circle.

When dealing with co-parenting narcissists, it may require a little more tact and strategy. For instance, PROVERBS 24:7 says: *Wisdom is too high for a fool: he openeth not his mouth in the gate.* The translation is this: when you operate with wisdom you paralyze the fool (narcissist).

When You're in a Position Like Sharing Children, and It's Necessary to Encounter Them, You Will Have to Insulate Your Soul.

By insulating your soul, we mean to cover your mind, will, and emotions so that they will have no impact on you. You'll physically be in the same space, yet, at the same time, you'll be in a different place emotionally.

COMMON SUGGESTIONS

A. CONTROL THE CONVERSATION WITH AS FEW WORDS AS POSSIBLE

The Bible says in PROVERBS 26:4 *Answer not a fool according to his folly, lest thou also be like unto him.*

The ability to control your words keeps your emotions under control. One major key to insulating your emotions from a narcissistic encounter is to master yes and no responses. You must become comfortable with awkward silence. Do not feel the need to expand the conversation. The narcissist plays off of your words and manages your emotions with signals detected in your commentary. When you are silent or intentionally limited in your words, you confuse the narcissist.

B. KEEP IT STRICTLY BUSINESS— YOU *CANNOT BE FRIENDS!*

The Bible says in PROVERBS 22:24–25: *Make no friendship with an angry man; and with a furious man thou shalt not go: Lest thou learn his ways, and get a snare to thy soul.*

Do not attempt to be friends with someone who has caused you so much anguish. Keep your relationship confined to business only. You cannot afford to open yourself up for more abuse.

C. ANTICIPATE THE MANIPULATION MANEUVERS AND COUNTER

It is stated in PROVERBS 24:7 *Wisdom is too high for a fool: he openeth not his mouth in the gate.*

You must be wise enough to know what to expect from the narcissistic abuser. Their tactics are usually very predictable. You must anticipate their behavior and respond rather than react. When you know what you're walking into, you take control of the moment before you enter the encounter.

D. APPROACH THE ENCOUNTER FROM A SPIRITUAL PLACE AND NOT ONE OF ANGRY EMOTION

The Bible puts it like this, in ISAIAH 59:19: *So shall they fear the name of the Lord from the west, and his glory from the rising of the sun. When the enemy shall come in like a flood, the Spirit of the Lord shall lift up a standard against him.*

God will defend your heart if you rely on him. As long as you try to manage the situation yourself, God will not get involved. When you turn it over into His hands, He will stand up and fight for you. He will give you His power to withstand the temptation to reconnect.

4. DENOUNCE THE NEED FOR CLOSURE

Closure is the idea that I need something to be spoken or done to allow my mind to accept things as they are. When we are on a quest for closure, we are, in essence, searching for an answer to a primary question, "Why did this happen?" It's also the subconscious hope for remaining possibilities to rekindle the façade of a relationship we once participated in.

The greatest hook in perpetuating the bond is the idea of needing closure. This need for closure keeps the wound open.

It's Lunacy to Think That the Person Who Broke You Will Fix You. The Desire for Closure Is a Poisonous Hook.

As long as you are waiting on people to fix you, you negate the power of God. God is not going to partner with your offender to do His work. If you want God to heal you, turn to Him and forget the other madness.

The Bible says in PSALMS 34:18, *The Lord is nigh unto them that are of a broken heart; and saveth such as be of a contrite spirit.*

Your Closure Is in God.

Here's the reality: *Choosing to forgive is the closure*! Forgiveness is the act of releasing a person from any liability. This disconnects you emotionally, and it allows God to untie you spiritually.

The word of God records one of Jesus' most prolific lessons on forgiveness. It is found in MATTHEW 18:21– 22, which says, *Then came Peter to him, and said, Lord, how oft shall my brother sin against me, and I forgive him? till seven times? Jesus saith unto him, I say not unto thee, Until seven times: but, Until seventy times seven.*

Jesus is basically instructing Peter to make forgiveness a lifestyle. When he says to do seventy times seven in a day, He is simply communicating that a healthy person practices releasing offenders and moving forward in life. As long as you are in a state of bitterness, you are emotionally and spiritually anchored to this person. Forgiveness is not about them; it is about you.

I Forgive Because I Can't Afford the Soul Tie That Unforgiveness Creates.

One of my favorite texts is JOHN 20:23, which states: *Whose soever sins ye remit, they are remitted unto them; and whose soever sins ye retain, they are retained.*

Here is the Message Bible version: "If you forgive a person's sins, they are gone for good. If you don't forgive sins, what are you going to do with them?"

Here's the wisdom: If you don't release a person's sins, transgressions, or offenses against you, you are stuck with holding them in your heart. What can you do with a heart filled with offenses and pain? You may do nothing but deteriorate and fester.

5. FOCUS ON REBUILDING YOUR SOUL

The fifth step in the process is to intentionally rebuild your soul. In the process of a narcissistic, abusive relationship, your mind is twisted into knots. When you decide to break free, it is as tedious as untangling a knotted shoestring. It requires patience and intention to ultimately recover your soul's (emotional) health.

The Bible says in ROMANS 12:2: *And be not conformed to this world: but be ye transformed by the renewing of your mind, that ye may prove what is that good, and acceptable, and perfect, will of God.*

The term *renewing* is speaking of renovating or remodeling your thinking. When experiencing narcissistic abuse, your brain becomes confused about your self-worth and your value. The self-perspective may become severely damaged. Some psychiatrists actually believe that long-term narcissistic abuse can damage the brain. Even if one has not endured enough trauma to create brain damage, a person is always emotionally reconstructed after a narcissistic relationship. This reconfiguration of the self-perspective, self-esteem, and worldview will always require the renovation of the mind.

In a renovation, there is the intentional tearing out of the things that do not serve the vision of the owner. There are usually large piles of trash that accumulate from the demolition. After the tearing out comes the introduction of the new and desired material. This is exactly what has to happen after a relationship with a narcissist. They have erected walls and filled the victim's head with inferior material in the form of thoughts. These things must be pulled down, thrown out, and replaced with healthy and profitable things. The soul must be rebuilt.

PRACTICAL STEPS TO REBUILDING YOUR SOUL

A. REMIND YOURSELF THAT YOU ARE NOT RESPONSIBLE FOR THIS PERSON'S FEELINGS, CONDITION OR FUTURE WELL- BEING

One of the very first things you will need to discard is the idea that you are responsible for the feelings of this narcissist. Every narcissist will subliminally transfer the belief to their victim that they are responsible for making the narcissist comfortable and happy. This is so deeply embedded that the victim may feel guilty for saving himself. The victim questions if they have done enough. You are not responsible for this person!

You Cannot Change This Person. You Must Leave Them in the Hands of God. He's the Only One Who Can Handle This.

B. FOCUS ON THE LESSONS OF THE EXPERIENCE AND NOT THE FEELINGS OF YOUR EMOTIONS

The soul tie or trauma bond created between you and this abuser stems from the emotion that has mutated your sense of reasoning. At this point, you must intentionally step into an objective position and take a realistic and intelligent view of what the transaction between you and this person has done for you. You will come back finding that they have done absolutely nothing but wreck your life and damage you emotionally.

When Your Soul Is Faced with the Reality of the Devastation This Person Has Created, It Will Attempt to Shift the Focus from the Facts Back to the Fantasy.

The fantasy consists of all of the false positives the victim ascribed to the narcissist in hopes that they could live up to it. The fantasy includes the lies the victim tells family and friends about how great of a person the narcissist really is. *Fantasy!*

It is important to consciously focus on the lessons of this experience because the tendency will be to get carried away with emotion. The emotion is the thing that has maintained the toxic bond thus far. You must move away from the emotion and reengage your logic. Take the lessons from this experience.

Do Not Waste Your Pain!

The psalmist wrote some very powerful words that serve us at this point. In PSALMS 119:71–72, it says: *It is good for me that I have been afflicted; that I might learn thy statutes. The writer acknowledges that there is value in pain and suffering, if we learn from it. Pain has to produce more than hurt, it is designed to produce learning and wisdom.*

What have you learned from this experience? What did you do wrong? What will you change? Pain presents a list of questions that should be answered; if answered accurately, the answers will point the way to freedom. If you don't take the lessons from this experience, you may enter into another relationship of the same nature.

Listen to the wisdom of the proverbs. In PROVERBS 17:10 it says: *A reproof entereth more into a wise man than an hundred stripes into a fool.*

In this text, the bible says that a person that doesn't learn from their hurts is foolish.

If You Don't Learn the Lessons and Change, You May Need to Redefine Yourself as a Volunteer Rather Than a Victim.

C. SUBMIT YOURSELF TO SOMEONE WHO KNOWS YOUR WHOLE TRUTH AND WILL HOLD YOU ACCOUNTABLE.

Do not for one moment think you are strong enough to resist yourself. There will be moments when the enemy, in the process, will be the person in the mirror. Those times when your flesh nature gets weak and is longing for certain experiences, you will need somebody who knows the whole truth and nothing but the truth to challenge you.

You are going to need accountability and counsel to pull yourself out of this snare. Somebody in your life has to take the liberty to tell you what you need to hear and not what you want to hear.

The word of God in PROVERBS 11:14 says, *Where no counsel is, the people fall: but in the multitude of counsellors there is safety.*

This is why the narcissist separates the victim from vital relationships. The plan was always to isolate you from accountability, wisdom, and protection.

D. FORCE YOUR LIFE FORWARD

Nothing moves forward by chance. Neither will your life move out of the parking-mode and into the drive itself without volition. You will have to choose to go forward and force your life out of the stagnant dysfunction of abuse. Even in a car, it never moves out of park into drive without an intentional and somewhat forceful act. No car slips into drive by accident unless it has a serious failure. Somebody chose to go forward.

You have the decision to make: Are you going to sit in pain or get up and move your life into your destiny? You cannot change what has been, but you have complete control over what will be. Are you going to park or are you going to drive? This is the question.

There's a powerful text recorded in ISAIAH 43:18– 19, which says: *Remember ye not the former things, neither consider the things of old. Behold, I will do a new thing; now it shall spring forth; shall ye not know it? I will even make a way in the wilderness, and rivers in the desert.*

The text admonishes the people through prophetic instruction to forget about what has been and to move forward with the expectation of a fresh move of God.

You must move forward in your thought life. You must move forward in your emotional life and redesign your everyday life so that it no longer resembles your former life with the abuser.

When your mind begins to revert back to old ways of thinking, forcefully jerk your consciousness to the new standard. Get rid of all paraphernalia representing the past. Create new circles and a whole new life. Begin to challenge your insecurities and step into your goals and dreams. Take the lessons you've learned and slowly begin to date again. When you recognize red flags, politely move on but live your life. Do not become a prisoner of a ghost of the past. Force your life forward.

CHAPTER 9

THE
POWER
OF
INDIFFERENCE

The greatest weapon you have against a narcissist or any self-absorbed person is your own indifference to their efforts to make every moment about them. The narcissist needs your attention and focus. When you do not seem to care, it creates confusion and injury for the narcissist.

To be indifferent is to show a lack of interest or concern about something intended to get a response from you. To be indifferent is to intentionally be nonchalant about everything concerning the narcissist. To be indifferent is to refuse to participate in the ongoing foolery of the narcissist.

INDIFFERENCE IS A MAJOR DEFENSE AGAINST A NARCISSIST

A primary marker of a narcissist is a person who has an unhealthy and excessive self-interest or self-admiration. This self-centered psychology creates an obsessive longing for the attention of others. When this need for being the focal point and controlling the emotional thermostat of their victim is disrupted, it confuses the narcissist's mind. Their sense of worth is largely wrapped up in their capacity to manage the will of others.

A Narcissist Is Either Seeking Attention or Seeking to Get Personal Needs Met at the Expense of Others.

The narcissist's lifeline is in people reacting or responding to their promptings. They're powerless to provide for themselves what they're leaching from their victim. Their energy is renewed by maintaining an emotional umbilical cord to their victim's soul. Without control over their victim, they're like a god with no worshippers or a king with no subjects. Indifference devastates the narcissist.

Jesus teaches us about the power of indifference with narcissists. Jesus dealt with religious narcissists in His entire ministry. These people were called Pharisees. When they were judging Jesus without cause, Jesus behaved indifferently. He did not allow them to get a rise out of Him.

The incident is recorded in MATTHEW 26: 61–63, where it says: *And said, This fellow said, I am able to destroy the temple of God, and to build it in three days. And the high priest arose, and said unto him, Answerest thou nothing? what is it which these witness against thee? But Jesus held his peace. And the high priest answered and said unto him, I adjure thee by the living God, that thou tell us whether thou be the Christ, the Son of God.*

Jesus simply ignored them by saying nothing. He seemed indifferent to the injustice and even the threat of death, which drove them crazy. When Jesus did respond, He responded sarcastically.

There's another time when Jesus used indifference to circumvent the trickery of a group of narcissists (Pharisees). They were trying to put Him in a legal trap and a state of public contradiction with calculated questioning.

This instance is found in JOHN 8:5–9, which says, *Now Moses in the law commanded us, that such should be stoned: but what sayest thou? This they said, tempting him, that they might have to accuse him. But Jesus stooped down, and with his finger wrote on the ground, as though he heard them not. So when they continued asking him, he lifted up himself, and said unto them, He that is without sin among you, let him first cast a stone at her. And again he stooped down, and wrote on the ground. And they which heard it, being convicted by their own conscience, went out one by one, beginning at the eldest, even unto the last: and Jesus was left alone, and the woman standing in the midst.*

The indifferent response of Jesus shamed them into moving on. Notice how the text says that Jesus acted like He did not even hear them. They sought a frustrated or maybe angry reaction from Jesus.

Jesus gifted them with His indifference. When they could not locate Him emotionally, Jesus shifted the advantage to Himself and used the occasion to embarrass and shame them with His statement— "He that is without sin should cast the first stone." Jesus' indifference foiled the plans of these toxic fellows.

INDIFFERENCE STRATEGIES

1. WHEN SOMETHING SHOULD MAKE YOU ANGRY, RESPOND CALMLY

You must view indifference as an emotional discipline. A great visual is to see it as maintaining your emotional thermostat controls inwardly instead of granting public access to your emotions.

Indifference Is Passive Resistance to Passive and Overt Aggression.

One of the main disciplines you will have to practice is responding calmly in situations that would normally make you react sharply.

The Bible says in PROVERBS 15:1, *A soft answer turneth away wrath: but grievous words stir up anger.*

The person who controls his words, tone, and temperament will control the encounter. It is intentional when a narcissist does things to anger or infuriate you.

When you give them a polar opposite response, you take power from them at that moment.

A Narcissist Feels a Sense of Control and Superiority When They Can, at Will, Control Your Blood Pressure.

This is why they bring you through continuous cycles of drama. It's never a steady ride; it's always a bipolar and manic-like experience. This is intentional. As long as they can stir you up, they know they are in control of the puppet strings.

The Bible teaches us a powerful life lesson. It states in PROVERBS 25:28: *He that hath no rule over his own spirit is like a city that is broken down, and without walls.*

The message of the text is that you are hopeless and defenseless when you cannot govern your internal world.

When you stop and think about it, many victims have been managed like a yo-yo for the entirety of the relationship because they had no control over the unction to react. The moment you can deliver an unexpected response is the day you begin to regain control and power.

2. AGREE WITH THEIR TWISTED LOGIC QUICKLY

"Yeah, you're right" will be your new go-to line. When the narcissist wants to get a reaction from you, they begin to say some of the most ridiculous things. They will make a stupid statement or accusation and then intently stare at you to measure your frustration. When you look at them with a wonderful smile and a steady glare and say, "You're right," it is even more befuddling than the calm response you gave them on the previous occasion.

Jesus teaches His disciples about responding to toxic people in MATTHEW 5:25. It says: *Agree with thine adversary quickly, whiles thou art in the way with him; lest at any time the adversary deliver thee to the judge, and the judge deliver thee to the officer, and thou be cast into prison.*

The point of Jesus' discussion is to defuse the situation at the lowest point rather than allow it to escalate to an unmanageable level.

Narcissists Live to Argue and Fight. When You Tell Them They Are Right; You Take the Fun Out of the Encounter.

Why argue with someone who will never see your perspective and will never admit the truth? This is a person who lives for conflict and despises resolution.

It gratifies them when you are constantly struggling to prove your point and to help them to see your perspective. It says, to them, that you are invested and care. It makes them feel significant and superior to you. But when you quickly agree with their lunacy, they become puzzled because you changed the rules of the game. The fun part was watching you sweat to convince them, and now you're not participating.

3. TAKE A WHILE TO RESPOND TO QUESTIONS OR ACCUSATIONS AND SOMETIMES NOT AT ALL

At certain points, the narcissist begins to berate their victim with a series of questions. They will question you about who you're talking to. They will accuse you of sneaking around with the neighbor. They will ask some of the most ridiculous questions and make some of the most outlandish and disrespectful accusations.

In some of these instances, you shouldn't dignify these antics with responses. Sometimes you should take a while to answer. Make them wait on a response. Never let your heart bleed before them. They do not deserve your vulnerability. At this point, the name of the game is "passive resistance meets passive aggression."

The Bible says in PROVERBS 29:11, *A fool uttereth all his mind: but a wise man keepeth it in till afterwards.*

When you speak your whole mind to a person you cannot trust, you have given them the steering wheel of your future. A narcissist will only ask questions when they want to gather information with which to control you or to simply drive you insane. Controlling your responses is the part that determines if they succeed in their plot or not.

In some cases, you'll just say I'm not sure, or I don't know. You must choose how, when, or if you answer their questions or respond to their accusations.

4. PLAY CRAZY

The narcissist will regularly do things to make you think you're losing your mind. This really works when you are oblivious to this tactic. Once you are awakened to the fact that this person is intentionally attempting to make you question your own sanity, you can then play the game from an even field.

When a Person Is Trying to Make You Believe That You Are Crazy, Play Crazy.

This tactic of pushing you to question your thoughts and reality is called gaslighting. The best way to respond to gaslighting is to act like you are completely not getting it. For instance, they may move your car from the garage to the street. Under normal circumstances, you would ask someone if they moved your car. You'd probably make a statement like this: "I know I'm not losing my mind." Once you're aware of what's going on, you just politely take your keys and go to your car like you believe it had always been on the street. When a person is trying to drive you crazy, act like you've already arrived. It will confuse and frustrate the narcissist. When they're playing checkers, you play chess. It won't only confuse them—it will quietly scare them. They may even begin to question themselves when none of their schemes moves you.

The Bible, once again, shines a bright light on a master key for living; it says in PROVERBS 24:7, *Wisdom is too high for a fool.*

It is a great deal of work to escape a narcissistic abuser. The only way to do so is to function at levels of wisdom that will transcend their diabolical schemes and plots.

Indifference Makes You Uninteresting to the Narcissist, and That's a Blessing.

CONCLUSION

This book has been a work of love. I have admitted that this subject matter is not an area of expertise for me. I became a student of narcissism because I encounter so many victims of narcissistic abuse.

The anguish and torment they exhibit motivated me to go deeper into the subject and explore the biblical context. My sincere hope is that the content of this offering has served to enlighten, confirm, and motivate the reader to pursue freedom and health.

A narcissist is never going to feel your position and make a choice to empower you. Their happiness clearly defines their world, and their will being the prime agenda. That is non-negotiable. You must accept that. When you know and accept these facts, you are then in a position to make the best decisions for yourself.

Let us be more conscious of how we raise our kids and manage our adult children. The last thing we should be guilty of is supplying the world with another narcissist because of emotional enablement or toxic parenting. Be the best parent you can, and train your children to be healthy and productive citizens.

It is also wise to remember that all narcissists are not created equal. Some are flamboyant, while others are angry and diabolical. You must analyze who you're dealing with to effectively and safely navigate your relationship with the narcissist. Ask the Holy Spirit to give you discernment, and just use your common sense.

One of the things that seem to be a great perplexity is the idea of biblical narcissists. The falsehood that the Bible is filled with perfect people is just a misunderstanding at best and a blatant deception at worst. The Bible is replete with every kind of narcissist one may discuss. Some of these biblical narcissists may serve as case studies for modern psychologists.

The intentional damage a narcissist does can only be described as demonic. Narcissistic abuse destroys the victim's self-esteem and self-confidence. Narcissistic abuse is so debilitating it may leave the victims with post-traumatic stress disorder. Some victims of narcissistic abuse never recover fully.

The most difficult relationship with a narcissist is to be married to one. Can you imagine what a miserable spouse a person makes who has no ability or interest in feeling their partner's hurt or concerns? That is a living hell. The narcissist lacks the fundamental empathy to make a decent spouse.

ME, MY, MINE

Everything with a narcissist is a game; it's always a game where they win or lose. The sad fact is that the narcissist is competing when others are unaware they are in any competition. The games they play are psychological and emotional. The goal is to break their victim emotionally.

Wisdom dictates that a person must have a strategy to exit the grip of a narcissist. Some narcissists won't let go easily. Some may become violent. The key is always to be three steps ahead.

The thing that I have found to be the secret weapon against a narcissist is the concept of indifference. It simply means to behave as though you do not care. When the actions and behavior of a narcissist land on a heart that clearly does not care, that person then takes the power from the narcissist. A victim's most powerful manoeuvre is to be empowered to say I do not care and then proceed to behave like it's true. When the chants of me, my, and mine are met with an indifferent stare or awkward quietness, the narcissist is discombobulated.

ABOUT THE AUTHOR

R.c. **Blakes Jr**. is a native New Orleanian. His persona is authentically New Orleans. R.C. was raised in the Black Church under the leadership of his late father, Bishop Robert Blakes, Sr. R.C. experienced a lot of emotional trauma as a young teen due to the rejection he experienced for being an unwed teen father. He learned early on how to navigate emotional pain alone.

R.C. eventually came into ministry as a preacher. As he grew and evolved, he began to realize that his ministry was different from that of the typical preacher. He had the vision to discuss all sides of life. He also had an idea to use platforms that preachers typically shun. As a consequence, he has reached people around the world with his messages and content. His books sell internationally every day.

R.C. and his wife, Lisa, have a passion to bring hope to the globe. To this end, they have extended his pastoral ministry—New Home Family Worship Center—to a global and digital platform. The name of the affiliate church is Cyber Church International. It is here that R.C. can minister to all races, creeds, and ethnicities under one umbrella of love.

R.C. has a bachelor's and master's degree in theology from the Christian Bible College of Louisiana, as well as an honorary doctorate from Saint Thomas Christian University in divinity. R.C. is also the author of several popular books and online programs.